D1070873

THE SELECTED LETTERS OF

THOMAS GRAY

Great Letters Series

LOUIS KRONENBERGER
GENERAL EDITOR

THE SELECTED LETTERS OF JOHN KEATS
EDITED BY LIONEL TRILLING

THE SELECTED LETTERS OF WILLIAM COWPER
EDITED BY MARK VAN DOREN

THE SELECTED LETTERS OF HENRY ADAMS
EDITED BY NEWTON ARVIN

THE SELECTED LETTERS OF THOMAS GRAY
EDITED BY JOSEPH WOOD KRUTCH

OTHER TITLES IN PREPARATION

THE SELECTED LETTERS OF LORD BYRON
EDITED BY JACQUES BARZUN

THE SELECTED LETTERS OF CHARLES LAMB
EDITED BY T. S. MATTHEWS

THE SELECTED LETTERS OF
LADY MARY WORTLEY MONTAGU
EDITED BY LOUIS KRONENBERGER

THE SELECTED LETTERS OF ANTON CHEKHOV
EDITED BY LILLIAN HELLMAN

THE SELECTED LETTERS OF SYDNEY SMITH
EDITED BY W. H. AUDEN

THE SELECTED LETTERS OF HENRY JAMES
EDITED BY LEON EDEL

THE SELECTED LETTERS OF GUSTAVE FLAUBERT
EDITED BY FRANCIS STEEGMULLER

THE

SELECTED LETTERS OF

THOMAS GRAY

EDITED WITH AN INTRODUCTION BY

JOSEPH WOOD KRUTCH

NEW YORK

FARRAR, STRAUS AND YOUNG, INC.

Manufactured in the United States of America

NOTE

The letters in this volume have been reprinted by permission of The Oxford University Press from the *Correspondence of Thomas Gray,* Edited by Paget Toynbee and Leonard Whibley (3 vols), 1935.

For the sake of brevity some of the footnotes have been reworded, without, however, affecting their essential meaning. To avoid the use of superior letters in abbreviations, as given in the original edition, modern abbreviations have been used here, and in some instances abbreviated words have been spelled out.

CONTENTS

INTRODUCTION

THOMAS GRAY was the only one of twelve children to reach adulthood. He himself lived into his fifty-fifth year and before he died he had become the most famous English poet of his generation. Yet his life was a series of retirements from what is commonly called living, and he seemed, during most of his time, to be accomplishing nothing.

All of his contemporary fame rested upon a little handful of poems, most of which were written during two brief periods. Today he is known also as one of the great letter-writers, but—as though by way of compensation—we have chosen to cherish ardently only one of the little handful of poems. In addition, the merits of two of the odes, "The Bard" and the "Progress of Poetry," are real and recognized, though no large public really takes them to its heart. In addition also, the ode on the "Death of a Favorite Cat" is admittedly charming, and the ode "On a Distant Prospect of Eton College" is the source of one sententious line—"Where ignorance is bliss, 'tis folly to be wise"—which everyone knows. But only the "Elegy Written in a Country Churchyard" really belongs in the first class of English poems. It has been as widely read and as widely loved as any other set of verses in our tongue.

This poem was completed in 1750, when Gray was in his thirty-fourth year, but it had been long a-polishing, and though the date when the first draft was written is not clearly established, one thing at least is certain. It was composed during a brief spurt—outburst would be too strong a word—of creative activity at the end of which Gray lapsed again into that mood of conscious futility which seems pitiful to some and merely exasperating to others, but which, in any event, was habitual with him. How easily, one cannot help thinking, something untoward might have happened at the moment when the "Elegy" was conceived, or how easily some one of the forces which operated could have failed to meet at the proper focus!

All poems are improbable, and no doubt opportunity does knock seldom, if not only once, to most people. But if this one knock had not come, or if Gray had not answered it, then perhaps the "Elegy" would not have been written; Gray would not have been remembered very widely; and we should have that hardly-to-be-imagined world in which no one had ever said, "The curfew tolls the knell of parting day," or, for that matter, any one of the score of other lines from the same poem which seem not so much to have been written as simply to exist.

Because he did compose, then polish over a period of years, and finally—when his hand was forced—actually cause the "Elegy" to be published, we have not only it and a few other poems, but also the letters, which were collected first because a great poet wrote them and which give Gray his second claim to fame. They have many of the virtues one takes almost for granted in letters from the eighteenth century. Besides that, they have also a special interest in what they half reveal and half conceal of the temperament and character of a very strange man who chose to lead a kind of life for which a good deal may possibly be said but which few have actually chosen to live so persistently. Presently something more will be said of the quality of the letters as letters, but for the moment we are concerned with them chiefly as the principal source of what we know about the man and how he lived.

The first, or at least the first documented, of those withdrawals which constituted Gray's life took place when he was admitted, through the kindness of his maternal uncle, to Eton College. One may assume that up to that time he had been unhappy enough, for he was the morbidly sensitive son of an eccentric, brutal, barely sane father who had so mistreated his mother, physically as well as in other ways, that she was finally compelled, in the absence of any sane divorce laws, simply to run away and to support herself by managing with her sister a London shop. At Eton her son began a retired, aloof little life of his own.

He was able to do so because the Eton of the eighteenth century was in some ways worse, and in some ways better, than it or the other great public schools became in their more familiar nineteenth-century heyday. It was worse because, like the eighteenth-century universities, it taught little except the bare bones of classical learning; because its atmosphere was barbarous rather than cultivated; and because the undisciplined pupils, after their four hours of classes, were left to their own devices—which included parties at the inn, expeditions to the races, a good deal of bullying, and a bed-time of their own choosing. It was better, because there was no nineteenth-century priggishness; little of what would now be recognized as "school spirit"; no compulsory games; and no conscious effort to force everyone into a mold.

What such a community could mean to another sensitive boy is plain enough to those who know the horror of the experiences which William Cowper carried with him throughout life. But there is no evidence that Gray suffered anything of the sort. He was let alone, and he formed with three other quiet boys what they self-consciously called the Quadruple Alliance, devoted to friendship, reading, and "sensibility."

One of the four, Thomas Ashton, grew up to be a rather vulgar, commonplace man of no great importance in Gray's history. Another, Richard West, though believed by his companions to be perhaps the real poetic genius of the group, died in 1742 and may thereby have provided the shock which released Gray's own poetic talent. The fourth was Horace Walpole, who was destined to remain, except for one interruption, one of the most important of Gray's correspondents and, in some respects, the most important person in his life.

Walpole, the son of the most powerful man in England, may seem an odd companion for the son of a poor shopkeeper. In some other respects they were almost equally ill assorted. At least in his young days, Walpole loved to mingle in his disdainful way with the members of that fast, fashionable world to which his birth gave him unquestioned access. Gray, though he was fond enough at one time of theaters and the opera, was never really comfortable when on even the fringe of smart society. Perhaps one should also say that the scholar, the pedant almost, which Gray was in part, made him a very different sort of man from the somewhat dilettantish Walpole. Something of the difference in the temperaments as well as in the fortunes of the two later made the difference between that exquisite and that college recluse which they respectively became.

In a schoolboy world the social differences were, however, less acutely marked and the temperamental differences had not yet developed very far. Moreover, there was one great kinship which was to hold good throughout life. Both were men who made, and who made early, The Great Refusal—by which is meant here the refusal to compete for the world's prizes, even for the least material of them. Walpole was to retire later to his play-castle, his printing press, and his *bibelots;* Gray to his college rooms. Neither was ambitious in any ordinary sense. Both, in a fashion which was sometimes almost dandiacal, resolved to strive with none because, so they professed at least to believe, none was worth their strife.

Already aloof at Eton, the members of the Alliance read Spenser, Milton, and Shakespeare; talked a great deal about the nature of friendship; and they gave one another romantic names—Gray was Orosmades, Walpole was Celadon. During vacations they exchanged carefully composed letters, and one, written by Gray in his eighteenth year to Walpole, is the earliest of his compositions to survive. It is included in this selection, where the reader will make what he likes of it. In less than a printed page there are three different literary allusions, one to *Henry IV,* one to Congreve's *Double Dealer,* and one to Cibber's *Love's Last Shift,* the allusion to this last making it, by the way, clear that the joke still current today in academic circles about the Frenchman who translated the title of the play into *La dernière chemise de l'amour* was already well known.

A few months after this letter was written, the members of the Quadruple Alliance were scattered when West left Eton for Oxford, Gray and Ashton for Cambridge. Six months later Walpole also became nominally a Cambridge undergraduate, though, being a young aristocrat, he spent most of his time in the world of London. During the next two years Gray wrote him often, sending accounts of life at the university, where drinking and smoking flourished and learning languished, among Fellows and students alike. A trip to London gave occasion for a report on plays and operas, a trip to Burnam for one on inns and roads. The earliest of those letters are couched still in schoolboy terms, but the last are less obviously affected, more mature.

The schoolboyish and the more mature are, however, alike in important respects. For one thing—and this was to remain true of all Gray's letters—they are not intimate outpourings of the heart but somewhat guarded literary compositions even at their most elaborately informal. Gray probably felt closer to Walpole than to any other human being except West, but the very romantic extravagance of his professions of regard makes them safely ambiguous so that they could, if occasion should arise, be discounted as mere polite badinage. These letters are also, like Walpole's side of the correspondence, sufficiently precious, sometimes sufficiently close to the mincing, to raise inevitably the question whether they could fairly be called effeminate, also.

Making all due allowance for the difference between eighteenth-century conventions and ours, one must admit that in Gray as well as in Walpole there was a good deal of what we call the feminine, if not the effeminate. Both were men of very delicate sensibilities living in a world where the typically masculine implied usually a coarseness which both found offensive. There was also something more to it than that, though probably not so much as some moderns will immediately conclude.

Homosexuality was common enough and well enough recognized in their time. There is, nevertheless, no evidence that either ever thought of himself as homosexual. What one feels is not that they were aware of, or even unconsciously influenced by, any positive sexual desire for other men, simply that they felt none for women either. Both were in a sense "mamma's boys," both the sons of women whose husbands were too rough for them, and both had lived in the domestic establishment of the mother, not the father. Peace, affection, and security were associated in their minds with a woman's world, not with a man's, and their affection for a mother separated from her husband tended to make them sexless.

Walpole's extraordinary tragic drama, *The Mysterious Mother,* makes it difficult to doubt that, in his case, his love for his mother had an unmistakable pathological aspect. The tone of Gray's letters to Mrs. Gray and the tone of his few references to her in letters to others is, on the contrary, so matter-of-fact and unemotional that one might suspect him of coldness did not what we know of his close association with her suggest another interpretation—namely that he did not dare permit himself any other tone. In any event there is no evidence that his feelings were as abnormal as Walpole's may, at moments, have been.

Nevertheless, in Gray's case also, the influence must have been extremely important. His sexlessness may not have been the cause of his retirement from the world but it made that retirement possible and it had also at least some effect upon his habits, his interests, and his tastes. He never had the means to indulge Walpole's feminine preoccupation with household furnishings and *bibelots,* but Gray also was unmistakably "fussy" and he was concerned with his own very modest household arrangements to a degree not usual in those bachelors who are such only by accident or force of external circumstances. Unlike Walpole he never, even in youth, went through the form or the pretense of the expected gallant affairs and when, years later, he wrote his friend Mason jocose letters about the latter's marriage he was so far outside his familiar fields that these letters contain almost the only examples of bad taste which could possibly be charged against him.

As the holder of a scholarship—twenty pounds a year—Gray

was obligated, as Walpole of course was not, to take his degree. Yet though he was destined to spend most of his life at the university, the disinclination to compete, to commit himself, to *do* anything definite, even to put an end to anything, be it a poem or a stage in his career, was already so firmly established that he got special permission not to take his degree. Both his parents had assumed that he would make law his profession, and while still an undergraduate he had been entered also at Inner Temple. But for the law he had no taste and he was saved the necessity of making any definite decision by Walpole's offer to take him, at Walpole's expense, upon a tour of Europe. Walpole was embarking upon the Grand Tour obligatory for all young men of birth and fashion. Who could be a more suitable companion than Gray? Gray accepted gladly, and so began what may be called the only adventure of his life. The two set out in March 1739; they visited France, Switzerland, and Italy; Gray returned, alone, in September 1741.

The immediate cause of this return was a quarrel between the two friends which is mysterious only in its accidental details, because it might have been confidently predicted from the beginning. Poor men are likely to be proud and to suspect offense from those who bestow favors; rich men take it unconsciously for granted that their wishes come first, and they sometimes expect a deference which they refuse to claim. Add that, in this case, there were important differences of temperament, and one may wonder that the two got along together as well as they did.

Walpole was less interested than Gray in the careful examination of antiquities, more interested in the fashionable society to which he had immediate access but into which Gray, who had little taste for it in any case, could be introduced only as his friend's protegé. As to the immediate cause of the rupture, Gray says nothing, and the hints which are to be found elsewhere lead to little more than further speculation. One story has to do with a letter allegedly opened by Walpole in order to test a suspicion that Gray was speaking unfavorably of him, and with Gray's resentment at this lack of trust and this breach of good manners. It makes little difference. But the rupture was not even nominally healed until after more than four years had passed.

Finally, and apparently through the efforts of an unknown lady, Walpole wrote offering reconciliation, and a meeting was arranged. Walpole later called the original fault his, and in the letters which later passed between the two, he seemed to have fewer reservations than his former friend about the genuineness of the reconciliation. But in a sense, the breach was never really healed. In future years they wrote one another often and were intimately associated in certain enterprises, but there were no more protestations on Gray's part of soul kinship.

The letters which Gray sent back from the Continent, mostly to Mrs. Gray, to West, and to Ashton, form an important section of his correspondence. In them he dutifully recorded the stages of his journey and described the official sights. Like most travelers in the days before Baedeker he sometimes devoted a little more space than we should to mere guidebook information. But that is by no means all he writes. His was a kind of sentimental journey, and what one gets is, among other things, the attempt of an intelligent and perceptive young man to discover what part of the visible past and the visible present has meaning for him. A lover of music, especially of Italian music, he compared critically what he heard in different cities and he passed his own judgments upon famous pictures.

Like most English travelers of the time he was no less impressed by the poverty in France and Italy than by the lavishness of public and private diversions. Thus in Paris: "There is not a house where they don't play, nor is any one at all acceptable, unless they do so too . . . a professed Gamester being the most advantageous Character a Man can have at Paris." Of Rome Walpole wrote in a joint letter: "Before a great number of years are elapsed, I question whether it will be worth seeing. Between the ignorance and poverty of the present Romans, every thing is neglected and falling into decay; the villas are entirely out of repair, and the palaces so ill kept, that half the pictures are spoiled by damp.—The cardinal Corsini has so thoroughly pushed on the misery of Rome by impoverishing it, that there is no money but paper to be seen. He is reckoned to have amassed three millions of crowns."

In the sixteenth and seventeenth centuries the principal reasons for visiting Italy had been to inspect its antiquities and (said the satirists) to acquire its vices. By Gray's time, scenery, especially "picturesque" or "sublime" scenery, was beginning to exercise its somewhat ambiguous fascination. To many earlier travelers the Alps had been merely a terrifying impediment to be overcome before the plains and the cities could be enjoyed. But Gray was to some extent a child of a new age, and perhaps the most famous of all his letters are one to his mother and one to West in both of which he describes his own feelings as he made the once dreaded crossing.

In the second he wrote "I own I have not, as yet, any where met with those grand and simple works of Art, that are to amaze one, and whose sight one is to be the better for: But those of Nature have astonished me beyond expression. In our little journey up to the Grand Chartreuse, I do not remember to have gone ten paces without an exclamation, that there was no restraining: Not a precipice, not a torent, not a cliff, but is pregnant with religion and poetry. There are certain scenes that would awe an atheist into belief, without the help of other argument. One need not have a very fantastic imagination to see spirits there at noon-day: You have Death perpetually before your eyes, only so far removed, as to compose the mind without frighting it."

Perhaps too much has sometimes been made of that passage by those who wish to represent Gray as a more typical, or at least a more highly developed, romantic than he actually was either in prose or in verse. It must be remembered in the first place that if his attitude was not as inevitable as it is today, neither was it completely unprecedented. John Evelyn, in the seventeenth century, had felt similar emotions, and Addison, earlier in Gray's own century, had analyzed the "agreeable horror" provoked by the spectacle of wild nature. In the second place, Gray had too deep-rooted a love of order and propriety to be a fully developed romantic, just as he had too little physical vigor or boldness to be an adventurer. The passage just quoted is hardly more significant than a sentence toward the end of the letter from which it was taken: "Mont Cenis, I confess, carries the permission mountains have of being frightful rather too far; and its horrors were accompanied with too much danger to give one time to reflect upon their beauties." Obviously this falls considerably short of the true Byronic rapture. Gray is still an eighteenth-century man calling for moderation in all things—even in sublimity.

One need not, on the other hand, explain away too much or fail to perceive how certain ideas already forming in the minds of his contemporaries find a genuine response in him, or how the phrases which he finds help to define these ideas. The opening contrast between the works of Nature and those of Art is not novel, but seems to be freshly felt. What is more important, Gray is moved to exclamation and, disregarding the counsel of Pope, he permits himself to "admire," not merely to "approve." He finds religion, not merely beauty, in the torrent and the precipice and the cliff, which, it should be noted, not only please the poet but also "confound the atheist." And when he says that "You have Death perpetually before your eyes, only so far removed, as to compose the mind without frighting it," he resolves the whole eighteenth-century paradox of the sublime. Here, as in his poems, Gray is a writer who has absorbed much that was new and that had a future in the history of English sensibility, but absorbed and integrated it without disrupting either his eighteenth-century mind or his eighteenth-century style.

In October 1742, very little more than a year after his return to England, Gray took the step which proved to be decisive and constitutes what might be called almost the last action he was ever to take as far as the ordering of his life was concerned. He returned to Cambridge (still technically an undergraduate) and was admitted as a "Fellow Commoner"—which meant, practically, that he now had indefinitely the privilege of living at the university, free and without duties. There he stayed, except for visits to London or the country. for the rest of his life, engaged in studies and diversions which, except for the few poems, came to nothing of any public importance. The same year that he retired to Cambridge his mother and her sister retired from the London shop to the village of Stoke Poges which he was to immortalize. Some twelve years later he got himself transferred from Peterhouse to Pembroke as the result of a mild practical joke which some boisterous young men attempted to play upon him. And in 1757 he declined an offer of the poet laureatship for the fastidious, possibly neurotic reasons given in the letter dated December 19 of that year.

Gray did not return to Cambridge because he had, or had any reason to have, a better opinion of its intellectual atmosphere than he had formed during his previous stay. He returned simply because the right to do so provided him with the opportunity, hardly to be hoped for anywhere else, of escaping every vestige of every sort of responsibility and of leading a life which seemed to him ideal. It may be that the death of West a few months before the step was taken had something to do with it, but one really needs no more than the temperament Gray had already exhibited to make his choice obvious. He was not always actually idle during his long years of retirement, but before anything is said either of his largely futile studies or of his mature personality and temperament it would perhaps be best to consider his production of a handful of immortal verses.

Gray was a reluctant poet as he was a reluctant everything else. Whether one calls it timidity, pride, disdain, or even the desire for perfection, something made him hesitate to write, hesitate to show what he had written, and hesitate above all to publish.

It is true that in youth he had sent occasional verses, translations, and squibs to members of the Quadruple Alliance; true also that he did a few college exercises. But the first poem whose publication he ever sanctioned (and that not until some years later) was an "Ode to Spring" sent to West on the day West died, June 1, 1742. Between about the middle of July and the middle of October of the same year he composed a sonnet to the memory of his friend, a "Hymn to Adversity," and the "Ode on a Distant Prospect of Eton College"—this latter being the first of his two poems indisputably still well remembered, in part at least.

For nearly five years after that he wrote nothing, or at least nothing which he cared to preserve.—Unless, indeed, he was already working on the "Elegy." Then, in May 1747, he sent Walpole the "Elegy on the Death of a Favorite Cat." Next month he appeared for the first time in print when Dodsley published the Eton ode at sixpence; a little less than a year later the same poem was published again when it appeared, together with the "Ode to Spring" and the "Elegy on the Death of a Favorite Cat," in a miscellany published by Dodsley. Then, in February 1751, the "Elegy Written in a Country Churchyard" was published. Next year he began to write "The Progress of Poetry," and in 1755 "The Bard." Ultimately two other unimportant poems, written earlier, were published. But after "The Bard" Gray wrote nothing else of which he sanctioned the publication except for two more poems added to the new edition of his *Poems* which Dodsley brought out in 1768.

The history of the "Elegy Written in a Country Churchyard" will throw what light can be thrown on his methods of composition, his attitude toward his own work, and upon a certain fussiness in regard to publication which suggests that the reluctance to commit himself to print was less simple modesty than an exaggerated fear of appearing ever so slightly unworthy or ridiculous.

Just when the first lines were put on paper is uncertain. Gray's friend William Mason had a copy of an early version, substantially different from the last, which he thought was written as early as 1742. On the other hand, Walpole, to whom Gray sent both an early and the final draft, thought the poem was not begun until 1745 or 1746. In any event, however, we know that it was completed by June 1750, when Gray sent a manuscript to Walpole with a letter in which he said, "Having put an end to a thing, whose beginning you have seen long ago, I immediately sent it to you." In other words this short poem had been at least four or five, possibly as many as seven, years in the writing.

Despite the long period of revision and polishing, Gray was, nevertheless, by no means ready to publish, and a letter to Walpole (February 11, 1751) tells the serio-comic story of how his hand was forced. The editors of a magazine had written him a letter informing him, with all the outward forms of deference, that they had in their possession the manuscript of a poem supposed to have been written by Gray and that they intended to print it. "I have," he wrote Walpole, "but one bad Way left to escape the Honour they would inflict upon me and therefore am obliged to desire you would make Dodsley print it immediately (which may be done in less than a Week's time) from your Copy, but without my Name, in what Form is most convenient to him, but in his best Paper and Character. He must correct the Press himself, and print it without any Interval between the Stanzas . . .—If he would add a Line or two to say it came into his Hands by Accident, I should like it better."

Two years later he was in even greater dither over the little volume of six poems which Walpole had arranged that Dodsley should print, with designs by Walpole's protegé Richard Bentley. Walpole, Gray protests, has promised Dodsley six odes and they aren't all odes. Then: "I am not at all satisfied with the Title. To have it conceived that I publish a Collection of *Poems* (half a dozen little Matters, four of which too have already been printed again and again) thus pompously adorned would make me appear very justly ridiculous." Positively, the volume must appear as "Designs by Mr. R. Bentley for Six Poems by Mr. T. Gray," *not* as "Poems by Mr. T. Gray with Designs by Mr. R. Bentley."

Finally, horror of horrors, Gray discovered that Dodsley intended a portrait of the poet by way of frontispiece. "Sure You are not out of your Wits! this I know, if you suffer my Head to be printed, you infallibly will put me out of mine. I conjure you immediately to put a stop to any such design. Who is at the Expence of engraving it, I know not; but if it be Dodsley, I will make up the Loss to him. The thing, as it was, I know will make me ridiculous enough; but to appear in proper Person at the head of my works, consisting of half a dozen Ballads in 30 Pages, would be worse than the Pillory. I do assure you, if I had received such a Book with such a frontispice without warning, I believe, it would have given me a Palsy."

Perhaps there is no such thing as modesty which is not in part a fear of disapproval. If there is any such pure modesty it was not Gray's. But it is hardly necessary for that reason to go, as some have gone, to the extent of accusing him of some monstrous, half-insane vanity or, in general, to forget, when describing his eccentricities, that few men appear sane when their lives are well documented.

Indeed, one may interpret Gray's reluctance to appear prominently before the public in terms which do not directly concern either modesty or vanity but which relate rather to his inclusive determination to be noncompetitive, to retire from normal life. Publication can hardly avoid being both competitive and, in some sense, exhibitionistic. It is asking for attention. Perhaps Gray felt, legitimately enough, that publication therefore did not quite become him, that it might lead to who knows what disruption of his plan of life. Perhaps, that is, he thought what a later, very different philosophical hermit thought when he rejected the offered gift of a door mat: "It is better to avoid the beginnings of evil."

Obviously, Walpole might almost be called Gray's literary agent; without him, Gray's few poems might never have been published at all. In exchange, Gray became a sort of research assistant for Walpole, consulting the libraries at Cambridge for bits of information which would throw light upon Walpole's collection of old pictures, medals, etc., or aid him in the compilation of his

Anecdotes of Painting in England. Meanwhile Gray was also cultivating a few other correspondents—notably Thomas Wharton and William Mason.

The first of these Gray had known before Wharton married and gave up his Pembroke fellowship to become a practicing physician. Gray's first surviving letter to him begins, "My Dear, dear Wharton (Which is a dear more than I give anybody else)," and they continued intimate friends up until Gray's death. A common interest in natural history as well as in Gothic decoration gave them other than purely personal topics, and one finds, for instance, Gray writing him at length about the purchase of "painted glass" for his windows and Gothic wallpaper.

William Mason was the clergyman-author (later Gray's literary executor and biographer) who wrote various plays and poems which enjoyed a certain celebrity in his own day. He regularly sent Gray his writings for criticism but sometimes found the detailed strictures he was offered rather hard to take. In addition to Wharton and Mason, various other correspondents were cultivated more or less assiduously over periods of varying length.

None of this, however, accounts for any large part of Gray's free time; and after the return to Cambridge he had nothing else. Part of it was spent nursing his melancholy and his gout, the symptoms of and remedies for which latter he meditated at length. Some more was passed playing a bit on the harpsichord or rereading favorite authors in the "good" editions which he cherished. A great deal, however, was spent in somewhat more strenuous activity, namely, in the compilation of notes, lists, and miscellaneous jottings on a great variety of subjects, some of which notes were intended for works vaguely planned though never executed, and a great many of which seem never to have had any purpose beyond themselves.

Gray professed to believe that the great remedy for melancholy was occupation. Perhaps the only way in which he could reconcile this belief with his reluctance to compete in the world of ambitious men was to perform labors which would never result in any publishable work. He filled the margins of his books with notes and he cited or referred to parallel passages in other writers. Into his commonplace books he transcribed verses or passages which pleased him, setting out proper names in red ink. He made alphabetical lists of all the poets of England, and of the armorial bearings of all the noble families. He collected notices of all the English cathedrals and made an author index for *The Greek Anthology.* Ruling papers into parallel columns, he headed each with the name of a wine known in antiquity and then under each listed the passages from classical writers which mentioned the one or the other. Then he did the same for olives, perfumes, articles of clothing, etc.

Having acquired early that interest in natural history which swept over Europe in the eighteenth century he interleaved a copy of Linnaeus' *System of Nature* and on these pages he made notes concerning English insects, and the like, which he could identify. He read Buffon as the volumes appeared; he annotated, also, Aristotle's *History of Animals* and various modern works. In addition he made a certain number of field observations and he kept, in column form, a record of temperature, phases of the moon, state of the weather, and so forth, with notes on the blooming and the ripening of fruits. But most of all this material, scientific or antiquarial, is unusable for any conceivable purpose.

In literature, in antiquities, and to some extent in natural history, Gray was a learned man. Boswell's friend William Temple called him the most learned man in Europe, and if that is a disputable statement at least his erudition was in a different class from that of a man like Walpole who could nevertheless make some public use of what he had learned. Gray might have written, before Thomas Warton, a history of English poetry; he might have anticipated, in Cambridgeshire, Gilbert White's *Natural History of Selborne.* But he did neither. He had, as his friend Mason was to write of him, banished the word "lucrative" from his vocabulary and he detested the thought that he might be considered an author by profession. Considering his compilations, one thinks inevitably of Francis Bacon's account of the three kinds of men of learning and inevitably one classifies Gray with the ants, with those who accumulate fragments which they merely heap up. Two or three poems make the grand exception. In them, like the bee, not like the ant, he transformed something into honey. Can one accuse of ineffectiveness or of waste a man who writes even one immortal poem?

Perhaps in some century before our own it would have been possible to say simply that Gray was a peculiar man who led a peculiar but nevertheless fruitful life and to let it go at that. The preoccupations and the convictions of today being what they are, one must at least acknowledge the inevitable question "What conditioned him?" Just how "neurotic" was he and how much evidence is there upon which to base legitimate speculation concerning the possible source of his neuroticism?

One may make some sort of answer to both of these questions on the basis of what has already been said. But there are also certain other things which may be added. Being an eighteenth-century man, Gray said that he was "melancholy," not that he was "neurotic." He mentions the fact often enough, but like another great contemporary victim of melancholy, Dr. Johnson, he follows the convention of his time which permits him to confess his misfortune but does not encourage him to analyze it at great length on the assumption that it is the most interesting thing about him. Had Swift, Johnson, Cowper, and Gray lived during the second half of the nineteenth or the first half of the twentieth century we probably should have had from them extended accounts of their obsessions and these obsessions would probably have constituted the principal *subject* of their literary work. As it is, what we have, instead, are writings which try to deal with the world outside the personality of the authors and which are merely colored by what was eccentric or unusual in their minds and temperaments.

At the age of twenty, Gray is already declaring that he is the victim of a hypochondria from which he never escapes. During all the rest of his life he complains from time to time of ills, physical as well as mental, and he distinguishes between what he calls the white melancholy and the black. The first, though it deprives its victims of the desire to laugh or to dance, does not prevent them from diverting themselves. It may produce, even, a rather agreeable sort of apathy. The other, the black, plunges the soul into absolute despair; and Gray has, he says, known both kinds.

Roger Martin, whose doctoral thesis, *Essai sur Thomas Gray,* is the most elaborately documented attempt to study Gray's temperament, piles little detail upon little detail until the unfortunate poet comes to seem almost a monster. He compares himself to the owl in his own garden. He declares that the truest likeness of himself is a zero. Mason describes him as a man in whom a combination of pride and timidity revealed itself in what appeared to be mere ill humor. He could be brusque with strangers and silent in company. He was morbidly fussy about his very simple domestic arrangements and, after an absence from Cambridge, he could send a long letter of instructions concerning the steps which must be taken to prepare his quarters for him. As he grew older his hypochondria grew more pronounced and so did certain obsessive fears—especially a fear of fire which led him to prepare what were regarded as comic arrangements for escape via the window and thus furnished the setting for the aborted practical joke which caused him to move in a huff from Peterhouse to Pembroke. He had also a sense of unworthiness and guilt which grew gradually worse until, near the end of his life, he considered resigning a professorship which had given him the first respectable income he had ever enjoyed.

Listed and elaborated in isolation as Roger Martin lists and elaborates them, these and other details compose into a picture at once pitiful and repellent. But many of the phrases from the letters which Martin uses to document the portrait seem to be somewhat overinterpreted and, perhaps because these letters are in a language not his own, Martin seems sometimes to miss the comic exaggeration in Gray's own statements. That he was neurotic is obvious; but if one can accept his "adjustment," his renunciation of the normal competitive life, then the minor symptoms are no more shocking than those met with again and again in biography. Whatever he may have said about his deadness, the letters are lively, and they certainly reveal a vivid interest in literature, in science, in friendship, and in gossip. They make, in sum, the very reverse of depressing reading. One certainly does not finish them with the positive conviction that their author did not often enjoy life in his own way.

Somewhat old-fashionedly, Martin seeks the ultimate source of Gray's peculiarities in the physical constitution of his possibly alcoholic father. It would be more up-to-date to lay more nearly exclusive stress upon his psychological environment, and speculation on the subject is at least harmless so long as one recognizes that, at such a distance, speculation is hardly more than speculation. When one remembers that Gray caused his mother to be described on her tomb as "the careful tender mother of many children, one of whom alone had the misfortune to survive her" one is tempted to make a possibly eccentric suggestion. Could it be, one asks, that the poet who knew that eleven brothers and sisters had died felt that early death was the proper fate of his tribe and dutifully refused to think of himself as anything more than a dubiously surviving shade?

More orthodox, of course, is the inevitable theory that Gray was simply a victim of that "mother fixation" for which circumstances had provided ideal conditions. And despite the unemotional tone of his letters to Mrs. Gray there is no doubting the strength of his attachment to her. He specifically provided in his will that he should be buried in his mother's tomb. In a letter written during his fiftieth year to his young friend Nicholls on the occasion of the illness of the latter's mother, he says, " . . . in one's whole life one never can have any more than a single Mother. You may think this is obvious and (what you call) a trite observation. You are a green Gossling! I was at the same age (very near) as wise as you, and yet I never discovered this (with full evidence and conviction, I mean) till it was too late. It is thirteen years ago, and seems but yesterday, and every day I live it sinks deeper into my heart." If Gray was made psychically but not physically sexless by his attachment to his mother and by his memory of her relations with her husband, then the inhibiting of one vital impulse may have had the effect it is said sometimes to have. He may have found it impossible to deny that impulse without denying at the same time many others and may have suffered from the unconscious conviction that in refusing sexual activity he must at the same time refuse almost all others.

But true as such a theory may be, true indeed as it probably is, one should guard against the assumption that it "explains" Gray. The most interesting things about him are the things which distinguish him from, not the things he has in common with, other victims of the mother fixation. Without it he no doubt would have been a different sort of writer even if he had been any sort of writer at all. But not every neurotic is a creative artist. It took more than a mother fixation to produce the "Elegy Written in a Country Churchyard." And any literary critic who forgets that fact would have been better off if he had never heard of modern psychology.

In the view of some, any "romantic" writer is, by definition, "neurotic," and to call Gray a neurotic, great or small, is therefore to introduce the vexed question whether he is or is not a "romantic" poet. On the one hand it may be pointed out that he persistently recommended Dryden as the best model for English poets to imitate and that Dryden is certainly no romantic. On the other hand it can be urged that in his own poetry appear an astonishing number of the subjects and attitudes which have been proposed as the criteria for romanticism. Like Walpole he was attracted by the Gothic, and some of his poems, notably "The Bard" and "The Descent of Odin," reflect strongly that interest in the Celtic past which expressed itself also in his antiquarian researches and in his excitement over the pseudo-ancient prose-poetry of "Ossian" Macpherson. Though he admired the odes of Dryden it may be said, nevertheless, that his own "Ode on a Distant Prospect of Eton College" differs from an ode by Dryden in the obvious respect that it is romantically personal, that it takes the poet himself as the real subject instead of being, in form at least, objective.

As for the "Elegy Written in a Country Churchyard," one can hardly deny that a predilection for twilight and melancholy, a preference for churchyards, for owls and for ivy, are all commonly thought of as romantic. Moreover, the concluding line of the first stanza, "And leaves the world to darkness and to *me*," will seem in itself decisive, since romanticism means essentially that the "me" of the poet takes the foreground. In the "Elegy," also, appears that idealization of the simple life, that respect for "the short and simple annals of the poor," which is related to the democratic movement and thus a manifestation of another aspect of romanticism.

By chemical analysis, then, Gray's best-known poems, including especially the "Elegy," are romantic. Yet the reader who considers the poems themselves rather than an analysis of them is likely to remain unconvinced, to feel that the label is misleading. Because both of something present and of something absent the effect is that of eighteenth-century classicism, not of nineteenth- or even eighteenth-century romanticism. One notices, of course, the diction of which Pope would have approved. One notices the abstract nouns, the capitalized personifications, the tendency to use specific details only as symbols of the general, the fondness for sententious moralizing, even the marked avoidance, in phrases like "the lowing herd," of what Pope would have called the "familiar" or the "low."

Even more important still, one is aware of intellectual convictions and of habits of mind and temperament which create an inescapably classical atmosphere. Gray was no materialist, for he was a Christian in the calm, secure "unenthusiastic" eighteenth-century fashion. But there is nothing mystical, at least nothing transcendental, in the "Elegy." It is everywhere stubbornly rational, even in its melancholy. The simple life, even the life close to nature, is good because it is healthful and free from great temptation, not because God dwells in a sunset. Gray has, if you like, something in common with Burns, something, though perhaps less, in common with Cowper. But he has little in common with Blake; much in common with Pope and with Thomson. And he is almost totally devoid of anything which suggests either the transcendentalism of Wordsworth, or Byron's no less irrational glorification of color and violence and fury for their own sakes. He is still moderate, still convinced that there is more truth in what some would call platitude than there is in paradox.

To say this is not to say that he has no flavor of his own, certainly not to say that his poetry is a mere collection of eighteenth-century commonplaces of vocabulary, thought, or feeling. His was an original sensibility and an original art. One may add that the originality involved at least a new stress on certain themes and emotions which was to persist and to be intensified in romantic art. But the essential fact is that Gray was not revolutionary in intention or in effect, that he was, and thought of himself as, continuous with an old tradition, not the maker of a new one. There was nothing explosive about his interests or his ideals. He could express everything which he had to express without disrupting the prevailing literary tradition.

In 1768 Gray was appointed Regius Professor of Modern History. The first letter in the concluding section of our selection is his reply to the Duke of Grafton, who had been authorized to make the offer. In effect the position was merely another, better-paid sinecure, though the professorship, when originally founded, had not been intended to be such. A little later Gray was queried in connection with a mild agitation provoked in Parliament by those who thought that Cambridge professors should be required to do *something* visible and he suggested that one public lecture a term might reasonably be expected. So far as is known, however, he himself never gave any, and he died three years after his appointment.

A final word may be said about the letters, which are the chief concern of this volume. They are deservedly among the most famous which have come down to us in English, and they have their special characteristics as well as certain characteristics common to the letters of their century. On the one hand they are not, like Walpole's, formal literary compositions. Except for a few written when he was very young and, perhaps, a few of those written from Europe, they are obviously intended for no eyes except those of the recipient. This does not mean that they are as casual and as formless as letters between friends often are today, because, in the eighteenth century, gentlemen did not exchange careless scrawls. It does mean, however, that they are much less self-conscious than Walpole's, almost as personal in their own different way as Cowper's. One reads them, as it were, over the shoulder of the person to whom they were addressed, not, as is often the case with Walpole's letters, with a full sense that the writer hoped we would someday be reading them.

The subjects are as various as Gray's own interests. There is quite a good deal about his mental and physical state, though, again like most eighteenth-century gentlemen, he had reserves which have since become unfashionable. There is even more about the theater, the opera, the new books, and the literary, historical, or antiquarian topics which interested him. There is also quite a good deal of gossip, and there are occasional glimpses into the political or fashionable world.

The pleasures which one gets from reading these letters are almost as various as the topics treated, but they are of two distinguishable sorts. One is the pleasure of meeting in some intimacy with a great and peculiar man whose thoughts and feelings, besides being interesting in themselves, are interesting for what light they throw on that great man. The other pleasure depends more upon the subjects treated than upon the reputation of the man who treats them. Many of the letters would be fascinating even though they were anonymous, for the simple reason that they make past events, past manners, and past ways of life real, as nothing else can. Hence to read them is to live for awhile in a century which had so much to recommend it.

LIST OF CORRESPONDENTS

COUNT FRANCESCO ALGAROTTI (1712-1764). An Italian scientist who visited London.

THOMAS ASHTON (1716-1775). One of Gray's three intimate friends at Eton. He later became a clergyman.

JAMES BROWN (1709?-1784). Fellow, and later Master, of Pembroke College, Cambridge.

JOHN CHUTE. An English gentleman whom Gray had met in Florence and whom he later visited in England.

JOHN CLERKE. A physician who had been one of Gray's fellow students at Cambridge.

JAMES DODSLEY (1724-1797). Younger brother of the following and engaged with him in the business.

ROBERT DODSLEY (1703-1764). Famous London bookseller and publisher.

AUGUSTUS HENRY, DUKE OF GRAFTON (1735-1811). Secretary of State through whom Gray was offered the Regius Professorship of Modern History at Cambridge.

MRS. DOROTHY GRAY (1691-1753). Mother of the poet. She lived at Stoke Poges, where the "Elegy" was written.

PHILIP GRAY (1676-1741). Father of Thomas Gray.

WILLIAM MASON (1725-1797). Poet and playwright whom Gray met in 1747. He became Gray's biographer and literary executor.

NORTON NICHOLLS (1742-1809). A clergyman whom Gray first met in 1762 but who became one of his closest friends.

WILLIAM PALGRAVE. Like Gray a Fellow Commoner at Cambridge, and one of his more intimate friends there.

RICHARD STONHEWER (1728?-1809). A Fellow of Peterhouse, Cambridge, with whom Gray was intimate. He was later appointed Historiographer to the King and he served as an undersecretary to the Duke of Grafton.

THOMAS WHARTON (1717?-1794). A physician and perhaps Gray's closest friend. They were already intimate while both were students at Cambridge. The two were often together, both in London and at Wharton's estate at Old Park.

HORACE WALPOLE (1717-1797). Son of the Prime Minister Sir Robert Walpole, famous as letter-writer, antiquarian, and dilettante. One of Gray's three intimates at Eton; his companion on the Grand Tour; and, except for the period of his quarrel, his lifelong friend.

RICHARD WEST (1716-1742). With Ashton, Walpole, and Gray formed the "Quadruple Alliance" at Eton. His early death profoundly affected Gray.

I

April 1734—January 1741

To HORACE WALPOLE

[*April 16, 1734*].

I believe by your not making me happy in a longer letter than that I have just received, you had a design to prevent my tireing you with a tedious one; but in revenge for your neglect I'm resolved to send you one five times as long: Sir, do you think, that I'll be fob'd off with eleven lines and a half? after waiting this week in continual expectation, & proposing to myself all the pleasure, that you, if you would, might give me; Gadsbud! I am provoked into a fermentation! when I see you next, I'll firk you, I'll rattle you with a Certiorari: let me tell you; I am at present as full of wrath & choler, as—as—you are of wit & good-nature; though I begin to doubt your title to the last of them since you have balked me in this manner: what an excuse do you make with your Passion-week & fiddle-faddle, as if you could ever be at a loss what to say; why, I, that am in the country could give you a full & true account of half a dozen Intrigues, nay I have an amour carried on almost under my window between a boar & a sow, people of very good fashion, that come to an assignation, and squeak like ten masquerades; I have a great mind to make you hear the whole progress of the affair, together with the humours of Miss Pigsnies, the lady's Confidente; but you will think perhaps I invent it, & so I shall let it alone: but I wonder you are not ashamed of yourself; in town, and not able to furnish out an epistle as long as a Cows tail! (excuse the rusticity of my simile) in short, I have tryed and condemned you in my mind, all that you can alledge to save yourself won't do; for I find by your excuses you are brought to your derniere Chemise; and as you stand guilty, I adjudge you to be drawn to the place of execution, your chamber; where taking pen in hand, you shall write a letter as long as this, to him, who is nothing, when not

your sincere friend
& most devoted humble Servant
T: GRAY.

To HORACE WALPOLE

[*Cambridge, Oct. 31, 1734*].

For Gods sake send me your Quære's, & I'll do my best to get information upon those Points, you don't understand: I warrant, you imagine that People in one College, know the Customs of others; but you mistake, they are quite little Societies by themselves: ye Dresses, Language, Customs &c are different in different Colledges:; what passes for Wit in one, would not be understood if it were carried to another: thus the Men of Peter-house, Pembroke & Clare-hall of course must be Tories; those of Trinity, Rakes; of Kings, Scholars; of Sidney, Wigs; of St Johns, Worthy men & so on: now what to say about this Terra Incognita, I don't know; First then it is a great old Town, shaped like a Spider, with a nasty lump in the middle of it, & half a dozen scambling long legs: it has 14 Parishes, 12 Colledges, & 4 Halls, these Halls only entertain Students, who after a term of years, are elected into the Colledges: there are 5 ranks in the University, subordinate to the Vice-chancellour, who is chose annually: these are [Masters, Fellows, Fellow-Commoners, Pensione]rs, & Sizers; The Masters of Colledges are twelve grey-hair'd Gentlefolks, who are all mad with Pride; the Fellows are sleepy, drunken, dull, illiterate Things; the Fellow-Com. are imitatours of the Fellows, or else Beaux, or else nothing: the Pension. grave, formal Sots, who would be thought old; or else drink Ale, & sing Songs against ye Excise. The Sizers are Graziers Eldest Sons, who come to get good Learning, that they may all be Archbishops of Canterbury: these 2 last Orders are qualified to take Scholarships; one of which your humble Servt has had given him: first they led me into the hall, & there I swore Allegiance to ye King; then I went to a room, where I took 50000 Latin Oaths, such as, to wear a Square Cap, to make 6 verses upon the Epistle or Gospel every Sunday morning, to chant very loud in Chappel, to wear a clean Surplice, &c. &c. Now as to eating: the Fellow-Com. dine at the Fellows Table, their Commons is worth 6*s*-4*d* a-week, the Pensioners pay but 2*s*-4*d*; if any body don't like their Commons, they send down into the Kitchen to know, what's for Sizing: the Cook sends up a Catalogue of what there is; & they chuse, what they please: they are obliged to pay for Commons, whither they eat it, or no: there is always Plenty enough: the Sizers feast upon the leavings of the rest; as to dress, the Fell. Commoners usually wear a Prunella Gown with Sleeves, a hat & no band; but their proper habit has its Sleeves trimmed with Gold-lace, this they only wear at publick Ceremonies; neither do the Noblemen use their pr. Habit commonly, but wear only a black Padesoy Gown: the Men of Kings are a sort of University by themselves; & differ in Customs from all the rest; every body hates 'em & when Almanzor comes to me, our Peoples stare at him, like a Lord-mayors Show, & wonder to see a human Creature among them: if I tell you, I never stirr out, perhaps you won't believe me; especially when you know, there's a Club of Wits kept at the Mitre, all such as come from Eton; where Alm. would introduce me, if I so pleased:—yet you will not think it strange, that I don't go abroad, when I tell you, that I am got into a room; such [a] hugeous one, that little i is quite lost in it; so [that] when I get up in the morning, I begin to travel [tow]ards the middle of it with might & main, & with much ado about noon bate at a great Table, which stands half-way it: so then, by that time, (after having pursued my journey full speed); that I arrive at the door, it is so dark & late, & I am so tired, that I am obliged to turn back again: so about Midnight I get to the bedside: then, thinks you, I suppose, he goes to sleep:

hold you a bit; in this Country it is so far from that, that we go to bed to wake, & rise to sleep: in short, those that go along the street, do nothing but walk in their sleep: they run against every Post they meet: but I beg pardon, for talking so much of myself, since that's not, what you care for—(To be continued)

To HORACE WALPOLE

[*Cambridge*] *23d Sunday after Trin.* [*Nov. 17, 1734*].

With care Carridge pade — **To mie Nuss att London** — **Present These**

Honner'd Nurse

This comes to let you know, that I am in good health; but that I should not have been so, if it had not been for your kind promise of coming to tend me yourself, & see the effect of your own Prescription: and I should desire of you, so please you, as how that, you would be so good as to be so kind, as to do me the favour of bringing down with you a quantity of it, prepared as your Grandmothers Aunt, poor Mrs Hawthorn (God rest her soul, for she was as well a natured, a good Gentlewoman, as ever broke bread, or trod upon Shoe-leather; though I say it, that should not say it; for you know, she was related to me, & marry! not a jot the worse, I trow) used to make it: now I would not put you to this trouble, if I could provide myself of the Ingredients here; but truly, when I went to the Poticaries for a drachm of Spirit of Ridicule; the saucy Jackanapes of a Prentice-Boy fleered at me, I warrant ye, as who should say, you don't know your Errand: so by my troth, away ambles me I (like a fool as I came) home again, & when I came to look of your Receipt; to be sure, there was Spt of RIDICULE in great Letters, as plain as the nose cn one's face: & so, back hurries I in a making-Water-while, as one may say, & when I came there, says I; you stripling, up-start, worsted-stocking, white-liver'd, lath-backed, impudent Princox, says I; abuse me! that am your betters every day in the week, says I; you ill-begotten, pocky, rascally, damned Son of a Bitch, says I —for you know, when he put me in such a perilous Passion, how could one help telling him his own—why, 'twould have provoked any Christian in the world, tho' twere a Dog—to speak; & so if you'll be so kind, I'll take care you shall be satisfied for your trouble: so, this is all at present from

your ever-dutifull & most
obedient & most affectionate,
loving God-daughter
PRU: OROSMADES

To HORACE WALPOLE

[*Cambridge, Jan. 27, 1735*].

Don't believe, that I would refuse to do anything for your sake, since at this present I am starving for you, & losing my dinner, that I may have the better opportunity of writing: you could not have given me a fairer occasion for shewing my obedience to your commands, than you have done in bidding me stay, where I am; for tho' before I was quite set upon coming to town, you give me so many reasons against it, that I am perfectly easy, & shall expect your coming with great resignation, that is, if you don't make it too long first: I read yesterday in the news, that Sir R. W.'s youngest Son, a young Gentleman of great hopes, was coming to Trinity-Colledge, Cambridge; pray, let me know, whither you are acquainted with him, & what hopes we may entertain of him; there are few here, but what give a good character of him, especially a long ungainly Mortal of Kings Col. & a little, waddling Fresh-man of Pet. House,[1] who pretend to be intimate with him: I can't see, how it should be; but however every body begins to envy the[m already; they are p]eople of very bad Repute; one of 'em is neither a Whig, nor a Tory, & the other passes for a Conjurer:—there is nothing to be seen in the Streets, at present, but new-made Batchelors, who walk to & fro, to shew their new Gowns; their examination is now over, during which time, they are obliged to set in the theatre for three days, from 8 in the morning till 5 at night without any fire; the first two days, they are liable to all

[1] Gray himself; he often alludes to his own diminutive stature.

the impertinent Questions which any Master of arts is pleased to ask them; they must answer every thing in Philosophy, which is proposed to them, & all this in Latin: the 3d day the first Moderator takes 'em out, half a dozen at a time into a Gallery atop of the theatre, in sight of every body, but out of hearing; he examines them again, as long as he will, & in what Sciences he pleases: the Junior-Moderator does the same thing in the afternoon; & then both the Proctors, if they have a mind; but they seldom do: the next day the Vice-chancellour & two Proctors tell them, whither they shall have their degrees, or not; & put on their Batchelours Gown & Cap: then they go all into the Schools, & one fellow belonging to each of the Colledges, gets into the Rostrum, & asks each of his Batchelours some strange Question: this was one, which was asked t'other day—Mi Filî, Domine, Domine N: quid est Matrimonium? The Answer was, Est conjunctio nunc copulativa, nunc disjunctiva. so then every body must laugh & the ceremony is ended. I tell you this, because it will be mine own Case some time or other, so I hope you will excuse me for tiring you with the account. and now, my dearest Hamlet, heaven send me safe from Wittemberg, or thee . . .
P.S. my letter last time was too late for the Post, so I hope you'll forgive it—

To HORACE WALPOLE

[*Cambridge, Feb. 4, 1735*].

I have so little to write, & so much to say; that, when you really do come, you may expect for the first fortnight to do nothing, but hearken to my Questions; & to spend the next month in answering them: nay, I assure you, I limit the time only that you may rest a while, to take breath; otherwise I could listen to you for the whole two years with an infinite deal of pleasure. I am forming the image to myself of your journey hither; I suppose you will come down Essex way, & if you do, first you must cross Epping forest, & there you must be rob'd: then you go a long way; & at last you come to Gog-magog hills, and then you must be overturn'd: I hope, you have not hurt yourself; but you must come at last to Foulmoor fields, & then you must fall Squash into a bog, pray, don't be fright-ed, for in about an hour and half you may chance to get out; now perhaps if it is not dark, you m[ay see the t]op of King's Chappel; tho' if it should be night, it is very likely, you won't be able to see at all: however at last you get into Cambridge, all bemudded & tired, with three wheels and a half to the coach, four horses lame, and two blind: the first thing, that appears, is a row of Alms-houses, & presently on the right-hand you'll see a thing like two Presbyterian Meeting-houses with the backside of a little Church between them, & here you must find out by Sympathy, that this is Peter-house, & that I am but a little way off, I shall soon feel how near you are; then you should say—no, no, I should say—but I believe I shall be too much overjoy'd to say anything, well; be that, as it will, I still hope, you will be almost as much so: dear Sir, you are welcome to Cambridge; what d'ye think? Pilk Hale about 3 months ago had a great inclination to visit Malepert, but thought it would not be well-bred not to let him know it beforehand; & being at a loss, who he should send; I persuaded him to go him-self, & let him know Mr. Hale would wait upon him in the after-noon. and so he did: Mal. promised to return it very soon; & ever since the other has staid at home with all his fine things set out to the best advantage, & is quite sure he'll come, & expects him every hour.

To RICHARD WEST

[*c. Dec. 20, 1735*].

Permit me again to write to you, though I have so long neglected my duty, and forgive my brevity, when I tell you it is occasioned wholly by the hurry I am in to get to a place where I expect to meet with no other pleasure than the sight of you; for I am pre-paring for London in a few days at furthest. I do not wonder in the least at your frequent blaming my indolence, it ought rather to be called ingratitude, and I am obliged to your goodness for softening so harsh an appellation. When you have seen one of my days, you have seen a whole year of my life; they go round and round like the blind horse in the mill, only he has the satisfaction of fancying he makes a progress, and gets some ground; my eyes are open enough to see the same dull prospect, and to know that having made four-and-twenty steps more, I shall be just where I was; I may, better than most people, say my life is but a span, were I not afraid lest you should not believe that a person so short-lived could write even so long a letter as this; in short, I believe I must not send you the history of my own time, till I can send you that also of the reformation. However, as the most undeserving people in the world must sure have the vanity to wish somebody had a regard for them, so I need not wonder at my own, in being pleased that you care about me. You need not doubt, therefore, of having a first row in the front box of my little heart, and I believe you are not in danger of being crouded there; it is asking you to an old play, indeed, but you will be candid enough to excuse the whole piece for the sake of a few tolerable lines.

To HORACE WALPOLE

March 11 [*1736*]—*Cambridge.*

Mr Dearest Horace

I was obliged by an unexpected accident to defer my journey somewhat longer than Monday, tho' it gave not at all the more time for pleasure, if it had, I should have been at the Masquerade with you: Ashton terrifies me with telling me, that according to his latest Advices we are to remain in a State of Separation from you the Lord knows how much longer; we are inconsolable at the News, & weep our half Pint apiece every day about it; if you don't make more haste, instead of us you may chance to find a couple of Fountains by your fireside: if that should be our fate I begg I may have the Honour of washing your hands, & filling your Tea-kettle every morning. . . .

To HORACE WALPOLE

[*July 15, 1736*].

Dear Sir

I sympathize with you in the Sufferings, which you forsee are coming upon you; we are both at present, I imagine, in no very agreeable situation; for my own part I am under the misfortune of having nothing to do, but it is a misfortune, which, thank my Stars, I can pretty well bear; You are in a Confusion of Wine & Bawdy & Hunting & Tobacco; & heaven be praised, you too can pretty well bear it; while our evils are no more, I believe we sha'nt much repine; I imagine however you'll rather chuse to converse with the living Dead, that adorn the Walls of your Apartments, than with the Dead living, that deck the middles of them, & prefer a picture of Still-life to the realities of a noisy one; & I guess, will learn to imitate them, and for an hour or two at noon, will stick yourself up as formal, as if you had been fixed in your Frame for these hundred years with an upright Pink in one hand, & a great Seal-ring in the other: I know nothing, but that the Judges were all blown up yesterday in Westminster-hall by some unlucky boy, that had affixed a parcel of Squibs & Crackers to several Acts of parliament, whose ruins were scatter'd about the hall with a great noise & displosion; it set the Lord Chancellour a laughing, & frighted every body else out of their senses, and Lord Hardwick order'd the grand Jury to represent it as a libel; yes! I know besides, that I shall be always yours. . . .

To HORACE WALPOLE

Here am I, a little happy to think, I sha'nt take Degree's; and really, now I know there is no occasion, I don't know but I may read a little Philosophy; it is sufficient to make a thing agreeable, not to have much need of it: such is my humour, but let that pass: West sup'd with me the night before I came out of town; we both fancied at first, we had a great many things to say to one another; but when it came to the push, I found, I had forgot all I intended to say, & stood upon Punctilio's and would not speak first, & so we parted: Cole has been examined by the Proctors, & took Bachelour's degree's, in order (he says) when he is Master of Arts, to assist a friend with his Vote & Interest; he told me he would not be puzzled in Philosophy, because he would not expose himself, but desired to be examined in Classicks, which he understood: he still talks of having his Leg cut off, & then being married: I have not seen Ashton; he is at St Ives, & I don't know when he comes back; Berkly makes a Speech the 5th of November; I am,

Dear, Dear Horace

Yours most truly,

T: G:

[Cambridge] Oct. 27 [1736]
when d'ye come

To RICHARD WEST

You must know that I do not take degrees, and, after this term, shall have nothing more of college impertinencies to undergo, which I trust will be some pleasure to you, as it is a great one to me. I have endured lectures daily and hourly since I came last, supported by the hopes of being shortly at full liberty to give myself up to my friends and classical companions, who, poor souls! though I see them fallen into great contempt with most people here, yet I cannot help sticking to them, and out of a spirit of obstinacy (I think) love them the better for it; and indeed, what can I do else? Must I plunge into metaphysics? Alas, I cannot see in the dark; nature has not furnished me with the optics of a cat. Must I pore upon mathematics? Alas, I cannot see in too much light; I am no eagle. It is very possible that two and two make four, but I would not give four farthings to demonstrate this ever so clearly; and if these be the profits of life, give me the amusements of it. The people I behold all around me, it seems, know all this and more, and yet I do not know one of them who inspires me with any ambition of being like him. Surely it was of this place, now Cambridge, but formerly known by the name of Babylon, that the prophet spoke when he said, 'the wild beasts of the desert shall dwell there, and their houses shall be full of doleful creatures, and owls shall build there, and satyrs shall dance there; their forts and towers shall be a den for ever, a joy of wild asses; there shall the great owl make her nest, and lay and hatch and gather under her shadow; it shall be a court of dragons; the screech owl also shall rest there, and find for herself a place of rest'. You see here is a pretty collection of desolate animals, which is verified in this town to a tittle, and perhaps it may also allude to your habitation, for you know all types may be taken by abundance of handles; however, I defy your owls to match mine.

If the default of your spirits and nerves be nothing but the effect of the hyp, I have no more to say. We all must submit to that wayward Queen; I too in no small degree own her sway,

I feel her influence while I speak her power.

But if it be a real distemper, pray take more care of your health, if not for your own at least for our sakes, and do not be so soon weary of this little world: I do not know what refined friendships you may have contracted in the other, but pray do not be in a hurry to see your acquaintance above; among your terrestrial familiars, however, though I say it that should not say it, there positively is not one that has a greater esteem for you than

Yours most sincerely, &c.

[Peterhouse, December, 1736].

To RICHARD WEST

I am coming away all so fast, and leaving behind me, without the least remorse, all the beauties of Sturbridge Fair. Its white bears may roar, its apes may wring their hands, and crocodiles cry their eyes out, all's one for that; I shall not once visit them, nor so much as take my leave. The university has published a severe edict against schismatical congregations, and created half a dozen new little procterlings to see its orders executed, being under mighty apprehensions lest Henley and his gilt tub should come to the Fair and seduce their young ones; but their pains are to small purpose, for lo, after all, he is not coming.

I am at this instant in the very agonies of leaving college, and would not wish the worst of my enemies a worse situation. If you knew the dust, the old boxes, the bedsteads, and tutors that are about my ears, you would look upon this letter as a great effort of my resolution and unconcernedness in the midst of evils. I fill up my paper with a loose sort of version of that scene in Pastor Fido that begins, Care selve beati.

[Cambridge] Sept. 1738.

To MRS. GRAY

[*Amiens, April 1, N.S. 1739*].

As we made but a very short journey to-day, and came to our inn early, I sit down to give you some account of our expedition. On the 29th (according to the style here) we left Dover at twelve at noon, and with a pretty brisk gale, which pleased everybody mighty well, except myself who was extremely sick the whole time; we reached Calais by five: The weather changed, and it began to snow hard the minute we came into the harbour, where we took the boat, and soon landed. Calais is an exceeding old, but very pretty town, and we hardly saw any thing there that was not so new and so different from England, that it surprized us agreeably. We went the next morning to the great Church, and were at high Mass (it being Easter Monday). We saw also the Convent of the Capuchins, and the Nuns of St. Dominic; with these last we held much conversation, especially with an English Nun, a Mrs. Davis, of whose work I sent you, by the return of the Pacquet, a lettercase to remember her by. In the afternoon we took a Postchaise (it still snowing very hard) for the Boulogne, which was only eighteen miles further. This chaise is a strange sort of conveyance, of much greater use than beauty, resembling an ill-shaped chariot, only with the door opening before instead of the side; three horses draw it, one between the shafts, and the other two on each side, on one of which the postillion rides, and drives too: This vehicle will, upon occasion, go fourscore miles a-day, but Mr. Walpole, being in no hurry, chooses to make easy journeys of it, and they are easy ones indeed;

for the motion is much like that of a sedan, we go about six miles an hour, and commonly change horses at the end of it: It is true they are no very graceful steeds, but they go well, and through roads which they say are bad for France, but to me they seem gravel walks and bowling-greens; in short it would be the finest travelling in the world, were it not for the inns, which are mostly terrible places indeed. But to describe our progress somewhat more regularly, we came into Boulogne when it was almost dark, and went out pretty early on Tuesday morning; so that all I can say about it is, that it is a large, old, fortified town, with more English in it than French. On Tuesday we were to go to Abbéville, seven teen leagues, or fifty-one short English miles; but by the way we dined at Montreuil, much to our hearts' content, on stinking mutton cutlets, addle eggs, and ditch water. Madame the hostess made her appearance in long lappets of bone lace and a sack of linsey-woolsey. We supped and lodged pretty well at Abbéville, and had time to see a little of it before we came out this morning. There are seventeen convents in it, out of which we saw the chapels of the Minims and the Carmelite Nuns. We are now come further thirty miles to Amiens, the chief city of the province of Picardy. We have seen the cathedral, which is just what that of Canterbury must have been before the reformation. It is about the same size, a huge Gothic building, beset on the outside with thousands of small statues, and within adorned with beautiful painted windows, and a vast number of chapels dressed out in all their finery of altar-pieces, embroidery, gilding, and marble. Over the high altar is preserved, in a very large wrought shrine of massy gold, the reliques of St. Firmin, their patron saint. We went also to the chapels of the Jesuits and Ursuline Nuns, the latter of which is very richly adorned. To-morrow we shall lie at Clermont, and next day reach Paris. The country we have passed through hitherto has been flat, open, but agreeably diversified with villages, fields well-cultivated, and little rivers. On every hillock is a wind-mill, a crucifix, or a Virgin Mary dressed in Flowers, and a sarcenet robe; one sees [not] many people or carriages on the road; now and then indeed you meet a strolling friar, a country-man with his great muff, or a woman riding astride on a little ass, with short petticoats, and a great head-dress of blue wool. . . .

To RICHARD WEST

Paris, April 12, 1739.

Enfin donc me voici à Paris. Mr. Walpole is gone out to supper at Lord Conway's, and here I remain alone, though invited too. Do not think I make a merit of writing to you preferably to a good supper; for these [eight] days we have been here, have actually given me an aversion to eating in general. If hunger be the best sauce to meat, the French are certainly the worst cooks in the world; for what tables we have seen have been so delicately served, and so profusely, that, after rising from one of them, one imagines it impossible ever to eat again. And now, if I tell you all I have in my head, you will believe me mad, mais n'importe, courage, allons! for if I wait till my head grow clear and settle a little, you may stay long enough for a letter. Six days have we been coming hither, which other people do in two; they have not been disagreeable ones; through a fine, open country, admirable roads, and in an easy conveyance; the inns not absolutely intolerable, and images quite unusual presenting themselves on all hands. At Amiens we saw the fine cathedral, and eat paté de perdrix; passed through the park of Chantilly by the Duke of Bourbon's palace, which we only beheld as we passed; broke down at Lusarche; stopt at St. Denis, saw all the beautiful monuments of the Kings of France, and the vast treasures of the abbey, rubies, and emeralds as big as small eggs, crucifixes, and vows, crowns and reliquaries, of inestimable value; but of all their curiosities the thing the most to our tastes, and which they indeed do the justice to esteem the glory of their collection, was a vase of an entire onyx, measuring at least five inches over, three deep, and of great thickness. It is at least two thousand years old, the beauty of the stone and sculpture upon it (representing the mysteries of Bacchus) beyond expression admirable; we have dreamed of it ever since. The jolly old Benedictine, that showed us the treasures, had in his youth been ten years a soldier; he laughed at all the reliques, was very full of stories, and mighty obliging. On Saturday evening we got to Paris, and were driving through the streets a long while before we knew where we were. The minute we came, voila Milors Holdernesse, Conway, and his brother; all stayed supper, and till two o'clock in the morning, for here nobody ever sleeps; it is not the way: Next day go to dine at my Lord Holdernesse's, there was the Abbé Prevôt, author of the Cleveland, and several other pieces much esteemed: The rest were English. At night we went to the Pandore; a spectácle literally, for it is nothing but a beautiful piece of machinery of three scenes. The first represents the chaos, and by degrees the separation of the elements. The second, the temple of Jupiter, and the giving of the box to Pandora. The third, the opening of the box, and all the mischiefs that ensued. An absurd design, but executed in the highest perfection, and that in one of the finest theatres in the world; it is the grande sale des machines in the Palais des Tuileries. Next day dined at Lord Waldegrave's; then to the opera. Imagine to yourself for the drama four acts entirely unconnected with each other, each founded on some little history, skilfully taken out of an ancient author, e.g. Ovid's Metamorphoses, &c., and with great address converted into a French piece of gallantry. For instance, that which I saw, called the Ballet de la Paix, had its first act built upon the story of Nereus. Homer having said he was the handsomest man of his time, the poet, imagining such a one could not want a mistress, has given him one. These two come in and sing sentiment in lamentable strains, neither air nor recitative; only, to one's great joy, they are every now and then interrupted by a dance, or (to one's great sorrow) by a chorus that borders the stage from one end to the other, and screams, past all power of simile to represent. The second act was Baucis and Philemon. Baucis is a beautiful young shepherdess, and Philemon her swain. Jupiter falls in love with her, but nothing will prevail upon her; so it is all mighty well, and the chorus sing and dance the praises of Constancy. The two other acts were about Iphis and Ianthe, and the judgment of Paris. Imagine, I say, all this transacted by cracked voices, trilling divisions upon two notes and a half, accompanied by an orchestra of humstrums, and a whole house more attentive than if Farinelli sung, and you will almost have formed a notion of the thing. Our astonishment at their absurdity you can never conceive; we had enough to do to express by screaming an hour louder than the whole dramatis personæ. We have also seen twice the Comedie Françoise; first, the Mahomet Second, a tragedy that has had a great run of late; and the thing itself does not want its beauties, but the actors are beyond measure delightful. Mademoiselle Gaussin (Mr. Voltaire's Zara) has with a charming (though little) person the most pathetic tone of voice, the finest expression in her face, and most proper action imaginable. There is also a Dufrêne, who did the chief character, a handsome man and a prodigious fine actor. The second we saw was the Philosophe marié, and here they performed as well in comedy; there is a Mademoiselle Quinault, somewhat in Mrs. Clive's way, and a Monsieur Grandval, in the nature of Wilks, who is the genteelest thing in the world. There are several more would be much admired in England, and many (whom we have not seen) much celebrated here. Great part of our time is spent in seeing churches and palaces full of fine pictures, &c., the quarter of which is not yet exhausted. For my part, I could entertain myself this month merely with the common streets and the people in them. . . .

To THOMAS ASHTON.

Dear Ashton,

You and West have made us happy to night in a heap of letters, & we are resolved to repay you tenfold. Our English perhaps may not be the best in the World, but we have the Comfort to know that it is at least as good as our French. So to begin. Paris is a huge round City, divided by the Seine, a very near relation (if we may judge from the resemblance) of your old acquaintance, that ancient river, the river Cam. Along it on either side runs a key of perhaps as handsome buildings, as any in the World. the view down which on either hand from the Pont Neuf is the charming'st Sight imaginable. There are infinite Swarms of inhabitants & more Coaches than Men. The Women in general dressd in Sacs, flat Hoops of 5 yards wide nosegays of artificial flowers, on one shoulder, and faces dyed in Scarlet up to the Eyes. The Men in bags,[1] roll-upps, Muffs and Solitaires. our Mornings have been mostly taken up in Seeing Sights: few Hotels or Churches have escaped us, where there is anything remarkable as to building, Pictures or Statues.

Mr. Conway is as usual, the Companion of our travels, who, till we came, had not seen anything at all; for it is not the fashion here to have Curiosity. We had at first arrival an inundation of Visits pouring in upon us, for all the English are acquainted, and herd much together & it is no easy Matter to disengage oneself from them, so that one sees but little of the French themselves.

To be introduced to the People of high quality, it is absolutely necessary to be master of the Language, for it is not to be imagind that they will take pains to understand anybody, or to correct a stranger's blunders. Another thing is, there is not a House where they don't play, nor is any one at all acceptable, unless they do so too . . . a professed Gamester being the most advantageous Character a Man can have at Paris. The Abbés indeed & Men of learning are a People of easy access enough, but few English that travel have knowledge enough to take any great Pleasure in their Company, at least our present Set of travellers have not. We are, I think to remain here no longer than Lord Conway stays, and then set out for Rheims, there to reside a Month or two, & then to return hither again. this is our present design & very often little hankerings break out, so that I am not sure, we shall not come back tomorrow.

We are exceedingly unsettled & irresolute, don't know our own Minds for two Moments together, profess an utter aversion for all

[1] A wig fashionable in the eighteenth century.

Manner of fatigue, grumble, are ill natured & try to bring ourselves to a State of perfect Apathy in which [we] are so far advanced, as to declare we have no Notion of caring for any mortal breathing but ourselves. In short I think the greatest *evil* [that] could have happen'd to us, is our liberty, for we are not at all capable to determine our own actions.

My dear Ashton I am ever

Yours sincerely

T: G:

Paris—Hotel de Luxembourg. Rue des petits Augustins
April 21, N.S. [1739].

To RICHARD WEST

Paris, [*c. May 15, and*] *May 22, 1739.*

After the little particulars aforesaid I should have proceeded to a journal of our transactions for this week past, should have carried you post from hence to Versailles, hurried you through the gardens to Trianon, back again to Paris, so away to Chantilly. But the fatigue is perhaps more than you can bear, and moreover I think I have reason to stomach your last piece of gravity. Supposing you were in your soberest mood, I am sorry you should think me capable of ever being so dissipé, so evaporé, as not to be in a condition of relishing any thing you could say to me. And now, if you have a mind to make your peace with me, arouse ye from your megrims and your melancholies, and (for exercise is good for you) throw away your night-cap, call for your jack-boots, and set out with me, last Saturday evening, for Versailles—and so at eight o'clock, passing through a road speckled with vines, and villas, and hares, and partridges, we arrive at the great avenue, flanked on either hand with a double row of trees about half a mile long, and with the palace itself to terminate the view; facing which, on each side of you is placed a semi-circle of very handsome buildings, which form the stables. These we will not enter into, because you know we are no jockies. Well! and is this the great front of Versailles? What a huge heap of littleness! it is composed, as it were, of three courts, all open to the eye at once, and gradually diminishing till you come to the royal apartments, which on this side present but half a dozen windows and a balcony. This last is all that can be called a front, for the rest is only great wings. The hue of all this mass is black, dirty red, and yellow; the first proceeding from stone changed by age; the second, from a mixture of brick; and the last, from a profusion of tarnished gilding. You cannot see a more disagreeable tout-ensemble; and, to finish the matter, it is all stuck over in many places with small busts of a tawny hue between every window. We pass through this to go into the garden, and here the case is indeed altered; nothing can be vaster and more magnificent than the back front; before it a very spacious terrace spreads itself, adorned with two large basons; these are bordered and lined (as most of the others) with white marble, with handsome statues of bronze reclined on their edges. From hence you descend a huge flight of steps into a semi-circle formed by woods, that are cut all round into niches, which are filled with beautiful copies of all the famous antique statues in white marble. Just in the midst is the bason of Latona; she and her children are standing on the top of a rock in the middle, on the sides of which are the peasants, some half, some totally changed into frogs, all which throw out water at her in great plenty. From this place runs on the great alley, which brings you into a complete round, where is the bason of Apollo, the biggest in the gardens. He is rising in his car out of the water, surrounded by nymphs and tritons, all in bronze, and finely executed, and these, as they play, raise a perfect storm about him; beyond this is the great canal, a prodigious long piece of water, that terminates the whole: All this you have at one coup d'œil in entering the garden, which is truly great. I cannot say as much of the general taste of the place; every thing you behold savours too much of art; all is forced, all is constrained about you; statues and vases sowed every where without distinction; sugar-loaves and minced-pies of yew; scrawl-work of box, and little squirting jets-d'eau, besides a great sameness in the walks, cannot help striking one at first sight, not to mention the silliest of labyrinths, and all Æsop's fables in water; since these were designed in usum Delphini only. Here then we walk by moonlight, and hear the ladies and the nightingales sing. Next morning, being Whitsunday, make ready to go to the Installation of nine Knights du Saint Esprit, Cambis is one: high mass celebrated with music, great croud, much incense, King, Queen, Dauphin, Mesdames, Cardinals, and Court: Knights arrayed by his majesty; reverences before the altar, not bows, but curtsies; stiff hams; much tittering among the ladies; trumpets, kettle-drums and fifes. My dear West, I am vastly delighted with Trianon, all of us with Chantilly; if you would know why, you must have patience, for I can hold my pen no longer, except to tell you that I saw Britannicus last Night; all the characters, particularly Agrippina and Nero, done to perfection; to-morrow Phædra and Hippolitus. We are making you a little bundle of petites pieces; there is nothing in them, but they are acting at present; there are too Crebillon's Letters, and Amusemens sur le langage des Bêtes, said to be of one Bougeant, a Jesuit; they are both esteemed, and lately come out. This day se'nnight we go to Rheims.

To MRS. GRAY

Rheims, June 21, N.S. 1739.

We have now been settled almost three weeks in this city, which is more considerable upon account of its size and antiquity, than from the number of its inhabitants, or any advantages of commerce. There is little in it worth a stranger's curiosity, besides the cathedral church, which is a vast Gothic building of a surprising beauty and lightness, all covered over with a profusion of little statues, and other ornaments. It is here the Kings of France are crowned by the Archbishop of Rheims, who is the first Peer, and the Primate of the kingdom: The holy vessel made use of on that occasion, which contains the oil, is kept in the church of St. Nicasius hard by, and is believed to have been brought by an angel from heaven at the coronation of Clovis, the first christian king. The streets in general have but a melancholy aspect, the houses all old; the public walks run along the side of a great moat under the ramparts, where one hears a continual croaking of frogs; the country round about is one great plain covered with vines, which at this time of the year afford no very pleasing prospect, as being not above a foot high. What pleasures the place denies to the sight, it makes up to the palate; since you have nothing to drink but the best champaigne in the world, and all sort of provisions equally good. As to other pleasures, there is not that freedom of conversation among the people of fashion here, that one sees in other parts of France; for though they are not very numerous in this place, and consequently must live a good deal together, yet they never come to any great familiarity with one another. As my Lord Conway had spent a good part of his time among them, his brother, and we with him, were soon introduced into all their assemblies: As soon as you enter, the lady of the house presents each of you a card, and offers you a party at quadrille; you sit down, and play forty deals without intermission, excepting one quarter of an hour, when every body rises to eat of what they call the gouter, which supplies the place of our tea, and is a service of wine, fruits, cream, sweetmeats, crawfish and cheese. People take what they like, and sit down again to play; after that, they make little parties to go to the walks together, and then all the company retire to their separate habitations. Very seldom any suppers or dinners are given; and this is the manner they live among one another; not so much out of any aversion they have to pleasure, as out of a sort of formality they have contracted by not being much frequented by people who have lived at Paris. It is sure they do not hate gaiety any more than the rest of their country-people, and can enter into diversions, that are once proposed, with a good grace enough; for instance, the other evening we happened to be got together in a company of eighteen people, men and women of the best fashion here, at a garden in the town to walk; when one of the ladies bethought herself of asking, Why should not we sup here? Immediately the cloth was laid by the side of a fountain under the trees, and a very elegant supper served up; after which another said, Come, let us sing; and directly began herself: From singing we insensibly fell to dancing, and singing in a round; when somebody mentioned the violins, and immediately a company of them was ordered: Minuets were begun in the open air, and then came country-dances, which held till four o'Clock next morning; at which hour the gayest lady there proposed, that such as were weary should get into their coaches, and the rest of them should dance before them with the music in the van; and in this manner we paraded through all the principal streets of the city, and waked every body in it. Mr. Walpole had a mind to make a custom of the thing, and would have given a ball in the same manner next week, but the women did not come into it; so I believe it will drop, and they will return to their dull cards, and usual formalities. We are not to stay above a month longer here, and shall then go to Dijon, the chief city of Burgundy, a very splendid and very gay town; at least such is the present design.

To PHILIP GRAY

Dijon, Friday, Sept. 11, N.S., 1739.

We have made three short days journey of it from Rheims hither, where we arrived the night before last: The road we have passed through has been extremely agreeable; it runs through the most fertile part of Champaigne by the side of the river Marne, with a chain of hills on each hand at some distance, entirely covered with woods and vineyards, and every now and then the ruins of some old castle on their tops; we lay at St. Dizier the first night, and at Langres the second, and got hither the next evening time enough to have a full view of this city in entering it: It lies in a very extensive plain covered with vines and corn, and consequently is plentifully supplied with both. I need not tell you that it is the chief city of Burgundy, nor that it is of great antiquity; considering which one should imagine it ought to be larger than one finds it. However, what it wants in extent, is made up in beauty and cleanliness, and in rich convents and churches, most of which we have seen. The palace of the States is a magnificent new building, where the Duke of Bourbon is lodged when he comes every three years to hold that Assembly, as governour of the Province. A quarter of a mile out of the town is a famous Abbey of Carthusians, which we are just returned from seeing. In their chapel are the tombs of the ancient Dukes of Burgundy, that were so powerful, till at the death of Charles the Bold, the last of them, this part of his dominions was united by Lewis XI. to the crown of France. To-morrow we are to pay a visit to the Abbot of the Cistercians, who lives a few leagues off, and who uses to receive all strangers with a great civility; his Abbey is one of the richest in the kingdom; he keeps open house always, and lives with great magnificence. We have seen enough of this town already to make us regret the time we spent at Rheims; it is full of people of condition, who seem to form a much more agreeable society than we found in Champaigne; but as we shall stay here but two or three days longer, it is not worth while to be introduced into their houses. On Monday or Tuesday we are to set out for Lyons, which is two days journey distant, and from thence you shall hear again from me.

To RICHARD WEST

Lyons, Sept. 18, N.S. 1739.

Scavez vous bien, mon cher ami, que je vous hais, que je vous deteste? voila des termes un peu forts; and that will save me, upon a just computation, a page of paper and six drops of ink; which, if I confined myself to reproaches of a more moderate nature, I should be obliged to employ in using you according to your deserts. What! to let any body reside three months at Rheims, and write but once to them? Please to consult Tully de Amicit. page 5, line 25, and you will find it said in express terms, 'Ad amicum inter Remos relagatum mense uno quinquies scriptum esto;' nothing more plain, or less liable to false interpretations. Now because, I suppose, it will give you pain to know we are in being, I take this opportunity to tell you that we are at the ancient and celebrated Lugdunum, a city situated upon the confluence of the Rhône and Saône (Arar, I should say) two people, who, though of tempers extremely unlike, think fit to join hands here, and make a little party to travel to the Mediterranean in company; the lady comes gliding along through the fruitful plains of Burgundy, incredibili lenitate, ita ut oculis in utram partem fluat judicari non possit; the gentleman runs all rough and roaring down from the mountains of Switzerland to meet her; and with all her soft airs she likes him never the worse; she goes through the middle of the city in state, and he passes incog. without the walls, but waits for her a little below. The houses here are so high, and the streets so narrow, as would be sufficient to render Lyons the dismallest place in the world, but the number of people, and the face of commerce diffused about it, are, at least, as sufficient to make it the liveliest: Between these two sufficiencies, you will be in doubt what to think of it; so we shall leave the city, and proceed to its environs, which are beautiful beyond expression; it is surrounded with mountains, and those mountains all bedroped and bespeckled with houses, gardens, and plantations of the rich Bourgeois, who have from thence a prospect of the city in the vale below on one hand, on the other the rich plains of the Lyonnois, with the rivers winding among them, and the Alps, with the mountains of Dauphiné, to bound the view. All yesterday morning we were busied in climbing up Mount Fourviere, where the ancient city stood perched at such a height, that nothing but the hopes of gain could certainly ever persuade their neighbours to pay them a visit: Here are the ruins of the Emperors' palaces, that resided here, that is to say, Augustus and Severus; they consist in nothing but great masses of old wall, that have only their quality to make them respected. In a vineyard of the Minims are remains of a theatre; the Fathers, whom they belong to, hold them in no esteem at all, and would have showed us their sacristy and chapel instead of them: The Ursuline Nuns have in their garden some Roman baths, but we having the misfortune to be men, and heretics, they did not think proper to admit us. Hard by are eight arches of a most magnificent aqueduct, said to be erected by Antony, when his legions were quartered here: There are many other parts of it dispersed up and down the country, for it brought the water from a river many leagues off in La Forez. Here are remains too of Agrippa's seven great roads which met at Lyons; in some places they lie twelve feet deep in the ground: In short, a thousand matters that you shall not know, till you give me a description of the Païs de Tombridge, and the effect its waters have upon you.

To MRS. GRAY

Lyons, Oct. 13, N.S. 1739.

It is now almost five weeks since I left Dijon, one of the gayest and most agreeable little cities of France, for Lyons, its reverse in all these particulars. It is the second in the kingdom in bigness and rank, the streets excessively narrow and nasty; the houses immensely high and large; (that, for instance, where we are lodged, has twenty-five rooms on a floor, and that for five stories) it swarms with inhabitants like Paris itself, but chiefly a mercantile people, too much given up to commerce, to think of their own, much less of a stranger's diversions. We have no acquaintance in the town, but such English as happen to be passing through here, in their way to Italy and the South, which at present happen to be near thirty in number. It is a fortnight since we set out from hence upon a little excursion to Geneva. We took the longest road, which lies through Savoy, on purpose to see a famous monastery, called the grand Chartreuse, and had no reason to think our time lost. After having travelled [two] days very slow (for we did not change horses, it being impossible for a chaise to go post in these roads) we arrived at a little village, among the mountains of Savoy, called Echelles; from thence we proceeded on horses, who are used to the way, to the mountain of the Chartreuse: It is six miles to the top; the road runs winding up it, commonly not six feet broad; on one hand is the rock, with woods of pine-trees hanging over head; on the other, a monstrous precipice, almost perpendicular, at the bottom of which rolls a torrent, that sometimes tumbling among the fragments of stone that have fallen from on high, and sometimes precipitating itself down vast descents with a noise like thunder, which is still made greater by the echo from the mountains on each side, concurs to form one of the most solemn, the most romantic, and the most astonishing scenes I ever beheld: Add to this the strange views made by the craggs and cliffs on the other hand; the cascades that in many places throw themselves from the very summit down into the vale, and the river below; and many other particulars impossible to describe; you will conclude we had no occasion to repent our pains. This place St. Bruno chose to retire to, and upon its very top founded the aforesaid Convent, which is the superior of the whole order. When we came there, the two fathers, who are commissioned to entertain strangers, (for the rest must neither speak one to another, nor to any one else) received us very kindly; and set before us a repast of dried fish, eggs, butter, and fruits, all excellent in their kind, and extremely neat. They pressed us to spend the night there, and to stay some days with them; but this we could not do, so they led us about their house, which is, you must think, like a little city; for there are 100 fathers, besides 300 servants, that make their clothes, grind their corn, press their wine, and do every thing among themselves: The whole is quite orderly and simple; nothing of finery, but the wonderful decency, and the strange situation, more than supply the place of it. In the evening we descended by the same way, passing through many clouds that were then forming themselves on the mountain's side. Next day we continued our journey by Chamberry, which, though the chief city of the Dutchy, and residence of the king of Sardinia, when he comes into this part of his dominions, makes but a very mean and insignificant appearance; we lay at Aix, once famous for its hot baths, and the next night at Annecy; the day after, by noon, we got to Geneva. I have not time to say any thing about it, nor of our solitary journey back again. . . .

To PHILIP GRAY

Lyons, Oct. 25, N.S. 1739.

In my last I gave you the particulars of our little journey to Geneva: I have only to add, that we stayed about a week, in order to see Mr. Conway settled there: I do not wonder so many English choose it for their residence; the city is very small, neat, prettily built, and extremely populous; the Rhône runs through the middle of it, and it is surrounded with new fortifications, that give it a military compact air; which, joined to the happy, lively countenances of the inhabitants, and an exact discipline always as strictly observed as in time of war, makes the little republic appear a match for a much greater power; though perhaps Geneva, and all that belongs to it, are not of equal extent with Windsor and its two parks. To one that has passed through Savoy, as we did, nothing can be more striking than the contrast, as soon as he approaches the town. Near the gates of Geneva runs the torrent Arve, which separates it from the King of Sardinia's dominions; on the other side of it lies a country naturally, indeed, fine and fertile; but you meet with nothing in it but meager, ragged, bare-footed peasants, with their children, in extreme misery and nastiness; and even of these no great numbers: You no sooner have crossed the stream I have mentioned, but poverty is no more; not a beggar, hardly a discontented face to be seen; numerous, and well-dressed people swarming on the ramparts; drums beating, soldiers, well cloathed and armed, exercising; and folks, with business in their looks, hurrying to and fro; all contribute to make any person, who is not blind, sensible what a difference there is between the two governments, that are the causes of one view and the other. The beautiful lake, at one end of which the town is situated; its extent; the several states that border upon it; and all its pleasures, are too well known for me to mention them. We sailed upon it as far as the dominions of Geneva extend, that is, about two leagues and a half on each side; and landed at several of the little houses of pleasure, that the inhabitants have built all about it, who received us with much politeness. The same night we eat part of a trout, taken in the lake, that weighed thirty-seven pounds; as great a monster as it appeared to us, it was esteemed there nothing extraordinary, and they assured us, it was not uncommon to catch them of fifty pounds; they are dressed here, and sent post to Paris upon some great occasions; nay, even to Madrid, as we were told. The road we returned through was not the same we came by: We crossed the Rhône at Seysell, and passed for three days among the mountains of Bugey, without meeting with any thing new: At last we came out into the plains of La Bresse, and so to Lyons again. Sir Robert has written to Mr. Walpole, to desire he would go to Italy; which he has resolved to do; so that all the scheme of spending the winter in the South of France is laid aside, and we are to pass it in a much finer country. You may imagine I am not sorry to have this opportunity of seeing the place in the world that best deserves it: Besides as the Pope (who is eighty-eight, and has been lately at the point of death) cannot probably last a great while, perhaps we may have the fortune to be present at the election of a new one, when Rome will be in all its glory. Friday next we certainly begin our journey; in two days we shall come to the foot of the Alps, and six more we shall be in passing them. Even here the winter is begun; what then must it be among those vast snowy mountains where it is hardly ever summer? We are, however, as well armed as possible against the cold, with muffs, hoods, and masks of bever, fur-boots, and bear skins. When we arrive at Turin, we shall rest after the fatigues of the journey. . . .

To MRS. GRAY

Turin, Nov. 7, N.S. 1739.

I am at this night arrived here, and have just set down to rest me after eight days tiresome journey: For the three first we had the same road we before past through to go to Geneva; the fourth we turned out of it, and for that day and the next travelled rather among than upon the Alps; the way commonly running through a deep valley by the side of the river Arc, which works itself a passage, with great difficulty and a mighty noise, among vast quantities of rocks, that have rolled down from the mountain tops. The winter was so far advanced, as in great measure to spoil the beauty of the prospect, however, there was still somewhat fine remaining amidst the savageness and horror of the place: The sixth we began to go up several of these mountains; and as we were passing one, met with an odd accident enough: Mr. Walpole had a little fat black spaniel, that he was very fond of, which he sometimes used to set down, and let it run by the chaise side. We were at that time in a very rough road, not two yards broad at most; on one side was a great wood of pines, and on the other a vast precipice; it was noon-day, and the sun shone bright, when all of a sudden, from the wood-side, (which was as steep upwards, as the other part was downwards) out rushed a great wolf, came close to the head of the horses, seized the dog by the throat, and rushed up the hill again with him in his mouth. This was done in less than a quarter of a minute; we all saw it, and yet the servants had not time to draw their pistols, or do any thing to save the dog. If he had not been there, and the creature had thought fit to lay hold of one of the horses; chaise, and we, and all must inevitably have tumbled above fifty fathoms perpendicular down the precipice. The seventh we came to Lanebourg, the last town in Savoy; it lies at the foot of the famous mount Cenis, which is so situated as to allow no room for any way but over the very top of it. Here the chaise was forced to be pulled to pieces, and the baggage and that to be carried by mules: We ourselves were wrapped up in our furs, and seated upon a sort of matted chair without legs, which is carried upon poles in the manner of a bier, and so begun to ascend by the help of eight men. It was six miles to the top, where a plain opens itself about as many more in breadth, covered perpetually with very deep snow, and in the midst of that a great lake of unfathomable depth, from whence a river takes its rise, and tumbles over monstrous rocks quite down the other side of the mountain. The descent is six miles more, but infinitely more steep than the going up; and here the men perfectly fly down with you, stepping from stone to stone with incredible swiftness in places where none but they could go three paces without falling. The immensity of the precipices, the roaring of the river and torrents that run into it, the huge craggs covered with ice and snow, and the clouds below you and about you, are objects it is impossible to conceive without seeing them; and though we had heard many strange descriptions of the scene, none of them at all came up to it. We were but five hours in performing the whole, from which you may judge of the rapidity of the men's motion. We are now got into Piedmont, and stopped a little while at La Ferriere, a small village about three quarters of the way down, but still among the clouds, where we began to hear a new language spoken round about us; at last we got quite down, went through the Pás de Suse, a narrow road among the Alps, defended by two fortresses, and lay at Bossolens: Next evening through a fine avenue of nine miles in length, as straight as a line, we arrived at this city, which, as you know, is the capital of the Principality, and the residence of the King of Sardinia. . . . We shall stay here, I believe, a fortnight, and proceed for Genoa, which is three or four days journey to go post.

To RICHARD WEST

Turin, Nov. 16, N.S. 1739.

After eight days journey through Greenland, we arrived at Turin. You approach it by a handsome avenue of nine miles long, and quite strait. The entrance is guarded by certain vigilant dragons, called Douaniers, who mumbled us for some time. The city is not large, as being a place of strength, and consequently confined within its fortifications; it has many beauties and some faults; among the first are streets all laid out by the line, regular uniform buildings, fine walks that surround the whole, and in general a good lively clean appearance: But the houses are of brick plaistered, which is apt to want repairing; the windows of oiled paper, which is apt to be torn; and every thing very slight, which is apt to tumble down. There is an excellent Opera, but it is only in the Carnival: Balls every night, but only in the Carnival: Masquerades, too, but only in the Carnival. This Carnival lasts only from Christmas to Lent; one half of the remaining part of the year is passed in remembering the last, the other in expecting the future Carnival. We cannot well subsist upon such slender diet, no more than upon an execrable Italian Comedy, and a Puppet-Show, called Rappresentazione d'un' anima dannata, which I think, are all the present diversions of the place; except the Marquise de Cavaillac's Conversazione, where one goes to see people play at Ombre and Taroc, a game with 72 cards all painted with suns, and moons, and devils and monks. Mr. Walpole has been at court; the family are at present at a country palace, called La Venerie. The palace here in town is the very quintessence of gilding and looking-glass; inlaid floors, carved pannels, and painting, wherever they could stick a brush. I own I have not, as yet, any where met with those grand and simple works of Art, that are to amaze one, and whose sight one is to be the better for: But those of Nature have astonished me beyond expression. In our little journey up to the Grande Chartreuse, I do not remember to have gone ten paces without an exclamation, that there was no restraining: Not a precipice, not a torrent, not a cliff, but is pregnant with religion and poetry. There are certain scenes that would awe an atheist into belief, without the help of other argument. One need not have a very fantastic imagination to see spirits there at noon-day: You have Death perpetually before your eyes, only so far removed, as to compose the mind without frighting it. I am well persuaded St. Bruno was a man of no common genius, to choose such a situation for his retirement; and perhaps should have been a disciple of his had I been born in his time. You may believe Abelard and Heloïse were not forgot upon this occasion: If I do not mistake, I saw you too every now and then at a distance among the trees; il me semble, que j'ai vu ce chien de visage là quelque part. You seemed to call to me from the other side of the precipice, but the noise of the river below was so great, that I really could not distinguish what you said; it seemed to have a cadence like verse. In your next you will be so good to let me know what it was. The week we have since passed among the Alps, has not equalled the single day upon that mountain, because the winter was rather too far advanced, and the weather a little foggy. However, it did not want its beauties; the savage rudeness of the view is inconceivable without seeing it: I reckoned in one day, thirteen cascades, the least of which was, I dare say, one hundred feet in height. I had Livy in the chaise with me, and beheld his 'Nives cœlo propè immistæ, tecta informia imposita rupibus, pecora jumentaque torrida frigore, homines intonsi & inculti, animalia inanimaque omnia rigentia gelu; omnia confragosa, præruptaque'. The creatures that inhabit them are, in all respects, below humanity; and most of them, especially women, have the tumidum guttur,[1] which they call goscia. Mont Cenis, I confess, carries the permission mountains have of being frightful rather too far; and its horrors were accompanied with too much danger to give one time to reflect upon their beauties. There is a family of the Alpine monsters I have mentioned, upon its very top, that in the middle of winter calmly lay in their stock of provisions and firing, and so are buried in their hut for a month or two under the snow. When we were down it, and got a little way into Piedmont, we began to find 'Apricos quosdam colles, rivosque prope sylvas, & jam humano cultu digniora loca'. I read Silius Italicus too, for the first time; and wished for you according to custom. We set out for Genoa in two days time.

To THOMAS WHARTON.

Proposals for printing by Subscription, in

THIS LARGE LETTER

The Travels of T. G. GENT: which will consist of the following Particulars.

CHAP. I.

The Author arrives at Dover; his conversation with the Mayor of that Corporation; sets out in the Pacquet-Boat, grows very sick;

---

[1] Goitre.

the Author spews, a very minute account of all the circumstances thereof: his arrival at Calais; how the inhabitants of that country speak French, & are said to be all Papishes; the Author's reflexions thereupon.

2.

How they feed him with Soupe, & what Soupe is. How he meets with a Capucin; & what a Capucin is. How they shut him up in a Post-Chaise, & send him to Paris; he goes wondring along dureing 6 days; & how there are Trees, & Houses just as in England. Arrives at Paris without knowing it.

3.

Full account of the river Seine, & of the various animals & plants its borders produce. Description of the little Creature, called an Abbé, its parts, & their uses; with the reasons, why they will not live in England, & the methods, that have been used to propagate them there. A Cut of the Inside of a Nunnery; it's Structure, wonderfully adapted to the use of the animals, that inhabit it: a short account of them, how they propagate without the help of a Male, & how they eat up their own young ones, like Cats, and Rabbets. Supposed to have both Sexes in themselves, like a Snail. Dissection of a Dutchess with Copper-Plates, very curious.

4.

Goes to the Opera; grand Orchestra of Humstrums, Bagpipes, Salt-boxes, Tabours, & Pipes. Anatomy of a French Ear, shewing the formation of it to be entirely different from that of an English one, & that Sounds have a directly contrary effect upon one & the other. Farinelli at Paris said to have a fine manner, but no voice. Grand Ballet, in which there is no seeing the dance for Petticoats. Old Women with flowers, & jewels stuck in the Curls of their grey Hair; Red-heel'd Shoes & Roll-ups innumerable, Hoops, & Paniers immeasurable, Paint unspeakable. Tables, wherein is calculated with the utmost exactness, the several Degrees of Red, now in use, from the riseing blush of an Advocate's Wife to the flameing Crimson of a Princess of the blood; done by a Limner in great Vogue.

5.

The Author takes unto him a Taylour. His Character. How he covers him with Silk, & Fringe, & widens his figure with buckram a yard on each side; Wastcoat, & Breeches so strait, he can neither breath, nor walk. How the Barber curls him en Bequille, & à la negligee, & ties a vast Solitaire about his Neck; how the Milliner lengthens his ruffles to his finger's ends, & sticks his two arms into a Muff. How he cannot stir, & how they cut him in proportion to his Clothes.

6.

He is carried to Versailles; despises it infinitely. A dissertation upon Taste. Goes to an Installation in the Chappel-royal. Enter the King, & 50 Fiddlers Solus. Kettle-Drums, & Trumpets, Queens, & Dauphins, Princesses, & Cardinals, Incense, & the Mass. Old Knights, makeing Curtsies; Holy-Ghosts, & Fiery-tongues.

7.

Goes into the Country to Rheims in Champagne. Stays there 3 Months, what he did there (he must beg the reader's pardon, but) he has really forgot.

8.

Proceeds to Lyons. Vastness of that City. Can't see the Streets for houses. how rich it is, & how much it stinks. Poem upon the Confluence of the Rhône, & the Saône, by a friend of the Author's; very pretty!

9.

Makes a journey into Savoy, & in his way visits the Grande Chartreuse; he is set astride upon a Mule's back, & begins to climb up the Mountain. Rocks & Torrents beneath; Pine-trees, & Snows above; horrours, & terrours on all sides. The Author dies of the Fright.

10.

He goes to Geneva. His mortal antipathy to a Presbyterian, &

the cure for it. Returns to Lyons. Gets a surfeit with eating Ortolans, & Lampreys; is advised to go into Italy for the benefit of the air. . . .

11.

Sets out the latter end of November to cross the Alps. He is devoured by a Wolf, & how it is to be devoured by a Wolf. The 7th day he comes to the foot of Mount Cenis. How he is wrap'd up in Bear Skins, & Bever-Skins, Boots on his legs, Caps on his head, Muffs on his hands, & Taffety over his eyes; he is placed on a Bier, & is carried to heaven by the savages blindfold. How he lights among a certain fat nation, call'd Clouds; how they are always in a Sweat, & never speak, but they fart. how they flock about him, & think him very odd for not doing so too. He falls flump into Italy.

12.

Arrives at Turin; goes to Genoa, & from thence to Placentia; crosses the River Trebia: the Ghost of Hannibal appears to him; & what it, & he say upon the occasion. Locked out of Parma in a cold winter's night: the author by an ingenious stratagem gains admittance. Despises that City, & proceeds thro' Reggio to Modena. How the Duke, & Dutchess lye over their own Stables, & go every night to a vile Italian Comedy. Despises them, & it; & proceeds to Bologna.

13.

Enters into the Dominions of the Pope o' Rome. Meets the Devil, & what he says on the occasion. Very publick, & scandalous doings between the Vines & the Elm-trees, & how the Olive-trees are shock'd thereupon. Author longs for Bologna-Sausages, & Hams; & how he grows as fat as a Hog.

14.

Observations on Antiquities. The Author proves, that Bologna was the ancient Tarentum; that the Battle of Salamis, contrary to the vulgar opinion, was fought by Land, & that not far from Ravenna. that the Romans were a Colony of the Jews, & that Eneas was the same with Ehud.

15.

Arrival at Florence. Is of opinion, that the Venus of Medicis is a modern performance, & that a very indifferent one, & much inferiour to the K. Charles at Chareing-Cross. Account of the City, & Manners of the Inhabitants. A learned Dissertation on the true Situation of Gomorrah. . . .

And here will end the first part of these instructive & entertaining Voyages. The Subscribers are to pay 20 Guineas; 19 down, & the remainder upon delivery of the book. N:B: A few are printed on the softest Royal Brown Paper for the use of the Curious. . . .

My Dear, dear Wharton

(Which is a dear more than I give any body else. It is very odd to begin with a Parenthesis, but) You may think me a Beast, for not haveing sooner wrote to you, & to be sure a Beast I am. Now when one owns it, I don't see what you have left to say. I take this opportunity to inform you (an opportunity I have had every week this twelvemonth) that I am arrived safe at Calais, & am at present at Florence, a city in Italy in I don't know how many degrees N: latitude. Under the Line I am sure it is not, for I am at this instant expireing with Cold. You must know, that not being certain what circumstances of my History would particularly suit your curiosity, & knowing that all I had to say to you would overflow the narrow limits of many a good quire of Paper, I have taken this method of laying before you the contents, that you may pitch upon what you please, & give me your orders accordingly to expatiate thereupon: for I conclude you will write to me; won't you? Oh! yes, when you know, that in a week I set out for Rome, & that the Pope is dead, & that I shall be (I should say, God willing; & if nothing extraordinary intervene; & if I'm alive, & well; & in all human probability) at the Coronation of a new one. Now as you have no other correspondent there, & as if you do not, I certainly shall not write again (observe my imprudence) I take it to be your interest to send me a vast letter, full of all sorts of News, & Bawdy, & Politics, & such other ingredients, as to you shall seem convenient with all decent expedition. Only do not be too severe upon the Pretender, &, if you like my Style, pray say so. This is à la Françoise; & if you think it a little too foolish, & impertinent; you shall be treated alla Toscana with a thousand Signoria Illusttrissima's. in the mean time I have the honour to remain.

Your lofing Frind tell Deth. T: Gray.

Florence. March 12. N.S. [1740].

P:S: This is à l'Angloise. I don't know where you are; if at Cambridge, pray let me know all how, & about it; and if my old friends Thompson, or Clark fall in your way, say I am extremely theirs. but if you are in town, I entreat you to make my best Compliments to Mrs. Wharton. Adieu, Yours Sincerely a second time.

To MRS. GRAY

Florence, March 19, 1740.

The Pope is at last dead, and we are to set out for Rome on Monday next. The Conclave is still sitting there, and likely to continue so some time longer, as the two French Cardinals are but just arrived, and the German ones are still expected. It agrees mighty ill with those that remain inclosed: Ottoboni is already dead of an apoplexy; Altieri and several others are said to be dying, or very bad: Yet it is not expected to break up till after Easter. We shall lie at Sienna the first night, spend a day there, and in two more get to Rome. One begins to see in this country the first promises of an Italian spring, clear unclouded skies, and warm suns, such as are not often felt in England; yet, for your sake, I hope at present you have your proportion of them, and that all your frosts, and snows, and short-breaths are, by this time, utterly vanished. I have nothing new or particular to inform you of; and, if you see things at home go on much in their old course, you must not imagine them more various abroad. The diversions of a Florentine Lent are composed of a sermon in the morning, full of hell and the devil; a dinner at noon, full of fish and meager diet; and in the evening, what is called a Conversazione, a sort of assembly at the principal people's houses, full of I cannot tell what: Besides this, there is twice a week a very grand concert. . . .

To MRS. GRAY

Rome, April 15, 1740. Good Friday.

To-day I am just come from paying my adoration at St. Peter's to three extraordinary reliques, which are exposed to public view only on these two days in the whole year, at which time all the confraternities in the city come in procession to see them. It was something extremely novel to see that vast church, and the most magnificent in the world, undoubtedly, illuminated (for it was night) by thousands of little crystal lamps, disposed in the figure of a huge cross at the high altar, and seeming to hang alone in the air. All the light proceeded from this, and had the most singular effect imaginable as one entered the great door. Soon after came one after another, I believe, thirty processions, all dressed in linen frocks, and girt with a cord, their heads covered with a cowl all over, only two holes to see through left. Some of them were all black, others red, others white, others party-coloured; these were continually coming and going with their tapers and crucifixes before them; and to each company, as they arrived and knelt before the great altar, were shown from a balcony at a great height, the three wonders, which are, you must know, the head of the spear that wounded Christ; St. Veronica's handkerchief, with the miraculous impression of his face upon it; and a piece of the true cross, on the sight of which the people thump their breasts, and kiss the pavement with vast devotion. The tragical part of the ceremony is half a dozen wretched creatures, who with their faces covered, but naked to the waist, are in a side-chapel disciplining themselves with scourges full of iron prickles; but really in earnest, as our eyes can testify, which saw their backs and arms so raw we should have taken it for a red satin doublet torn, and shewing the skin through, had we not been convinced of the contrary by the blood which was plentifully sprinkled about them. It is late; I give you joy of Port-Bello, and many other things, which I hope are all true. . . .

To MRS. GRAY

Naples, June [*14*], *1740.*

Our journey hither was through the most beautiful part of the finest country in the world; and every spot of it, on some account or other, famous for these three thousand years past. The season has hitherto been just as warm as one would wish it; no unwholesome airs, or violent heats, yet heard of: The people call it a backward year, and are in pain about their corn, wine, and oil. but we, who are neither corn, wine, nor oil, find it very agreeable. Our road was through Velletri, Cisterna, Terracina, Capua, and Aversa, and so to Naples. The minute one leaves his Holiness's dominions, the face of things begins to change from wide uncultivated plains to olive groves and well-tilled fields of corn, intermixed with ranks of elms, every one of which has its vine twining about it, and hanging in festoons between the rows from one tree to another. The great old fig-trees, the oranges in full bloom, and myrtles in every hedge, make one of the delightfullest scenes you can conceive; besides that, the roads are wide, well-kept, and full of passengers, a sight I have not beheld this long time. My wonder still increased upon entering the city, which I think, for number of people, outdoes both Paris and London. The streets are one continued market, and thronged with populace so much that a coach can hardly pass. The common sort are a jolly lively kind of animals, more industrious than Italians usually are; they work till evening; then take their lute or guitar (for they all play) and walk about the city, or upon the sea-shore with it, to enjoy the fresco. One sees their little brown children jumping about stark-naked, and the bigger ones dancing with castanets, while others play on the cymbal to them. Your maps will show you the situation of Naples; it is on the most lovely bay in the world, and one of the calmest seas: It has many other beauties besides those of nature. We have spent two days in visiting the remarkable places in the country round it, such as the bay of Baiæ, and its remains of antiquity; the lake Avernus, and the Solfatara, Charon's grotto, &c. We have been in the Sybils' cave and many other strange holes under ground (I only name them, because you may consult Sandy's travels); but the strangest hole I ever was in, has been to-day at a place called Portici, where his Sicilian Majesty has a country-seat. About a year ago, as they were digging, they discovered some parts of ancient buildings above thirty feet deep in the ground: Curiosity led them on, and they have been digging ever since; the passage they have made, with all its turnings and windings, is now more than a mile long. As you walk you see parts of an amphitheatre, many houses adorned with marble columns, and incrusted with the same; the front of a temple, several arched vaults of rooms painted in fresco. Some pieces of painting have been taken out from hence, finer than any thing of the kind before discovered, and with these the King has adorned his palace; also a number of statues, medals, and gems; and more are dug out every day. This is known to be a Roman town, that in the Emperor Titus's time was overwhelmed by a furious errup- tion of Mount Vesuvius, which is hard by. The wood and beams remain so perfect that you may see the grain; but burnt to a coal, and dropping into dust upon the least touch. We were to-day at the foot of that mountain, which at present smokes only a little, where we saw the materials that fed the stream of fire, which about four years since ran down its side. We have but a few days longer to stay here; too little in conscience for such a place. . . .

To MRS. GRAY

Florence, Aug. 21, N.S. 1740.

It is some time since I have had the pleasure of writing to you, having been upon a little excursion cross the mountains to Bologna. We set out from hence at sunset, passed the Apennines by moon-light, travelling incessantly till we came to Bologna at four in the afternoon next day. There we spent a week agreeably enough, and returned as we came. The day before yesterday arrived the news of a Pope; and I have the mortification of being within four days journey of Rome, and not seeing his coronation, the heats being violent, and the infectious air now at its height. We had an instance, the other day, that it is not only fancy. Two country fellows, strong men, and used to the country about Rome, having occasion to come from thence hither, and travelling on foot, as common with them, one died suddenly on the road; the other got hither, but extremely weak, and in a manner stupid; he was carried to the hospital, but died in two days. So, between fear and laziness, we remain here, and must be satisfied with the accounts other people give us of the matter. The new Pope is called Benedict XIV. being created Cardinal by Benedict XIII. the last Pope but one. His name is Lambertini, a noble Bolognese, and Archbishop of that city. When I was first there, I remember to have seen him two or three times; he is a short, fat man, about sixty-five years of age, of a hearty, merry countenance, and likely to live some years. He bears a good character for generosity, affability, and other virtues; and, they say, wants neither knowledge nor capacity. The worst side of him is, that he has a nephew or two; besides a certain young favourite, called Melara, who is said to have had, for some time, the arbitrary disposal of his purse and family. He is reported to have made a little speech to the Cardinals in the Conclave, while they were undetermined about an election, as follows: 'Most eminent Lords, here are three Bolognese of different characters, but all equally proper for the Popedom. If it be your pleasures, to pitch upon a Saint, there is Cardinal Gotti; if upon a Politician, there is Aldrovandi; if upon a Booby, here am I.' The Italian is much more expressive, and, indeed, not to be translated; wherefore, if you meet with any body that understands it, you may show them what he said in the language he spoke it. 'Eminssimi. Sigri. Ci siamo tré, diversi sì, mà tutti idonei al Papato. Si vi piace un Santo, c' è l'Gotti; se volete una testa scaltra, e Politica, c' l'Aldrovandé; se un Coglione, eccomi!' Cardinal Coscia is restored to his liberty, and, it is said, will be to all his benefices. Corsini (the late Pope's nephew) as he has had no hand in this election, it is hoped, will be called to account for all his villanous practices. The Pretender, they say, has resigned all his pretensions to his eldest boy, and will accept of the Grand Chancellorship, which is thirty thousand crowns a-year; the pension he has at present is only twenty thousand. I do not affirm the truth of this last article; because, if he does, it is necessary he should take the ecclesiastical habit, and it will sound mighty odd to be called his Majesty the Chancellor.—So ends my Gazette.

To PHILIP GRAY

Florence, Oct. 9, 1740.

The beginning of next spring is the time determined for our return at furthest; possibly it may be before that time. How the interim will be employed, or what route we shall take, is not so certain. If we remain friends with France, upon leaving this country we shall cross over to Venice, and so return through the cities north of the Po to Genoa; from thence take a felucca to Marseilles, and come back through Paris. If the contrary fall out, which seems not unlikely, we must make the Milanese, and those parts of Italy, in our way to Venice; from thence pass through the Tirol into Germany, and come home by the Low-Countries. As for Florence, it has been gayer than ordinary for this last month, being one round of balls and entertainments, occasioned by the arrival of a great Milanese Lady; for the only thing the Italians shine in, is their reception of strangers. At such times every thing is magnificence: The more remarkable, as in their ordinary course of life they are parsimonious, even to a degree of nastiness. I saw in one of the vastest palaces in Rome (that of Prince Pamfilio) the apartment which he himself inhabited, a bed that most servants in England would disdain to lie in, and furniture much like that of a soph at Cambridge, for convenience and neatness. This man is worth 30,000*l.* sterling a year. As for eating, there are not two Cardinals in Rome that allow more than six paoli, which is three shillings a day, for the expence of their table; and you may imagine they are still less extravagant here than there. But when they receive a visit from any friend, their houses and persons are set out to the greatest advantage, and appear in all their splendour; it is, indeed, from a motive of vanity, and with the hopes of having it repaid them with interest, whenever they have occasion to return the visit. I call visits going from one city of Italy to another; for it is not so among acquaintance of the same place on common occasions. The new Pope has retrenched the charges of his own table to a sequin (10s.) a meal. The applause which all he says and does meets with, is enough to encourage him really to deserve fame. They say he is an able and honest man; he is reckoned a wit too. The other day, when the Senator of Rome came to wait upon him, at the first compliments he made him the Pope pulled off his cap: His Master of the Ceremonies, who stood by his side, touched him softly, as to warn him that such a condescension was too great in him, and out of all manner of rule: Upon which he turned to him and said, 'Oh! I cry you mercy, good Master, it is true, I am but a Novice of a Pope; I have not yet so much as learned ill manners.' . . .

To PHILIP GRAY

Florence, Jan. 12, 1741.

We still continue constant at Florence, at present one of the dullest cities in Italy. Though it is the middle of the Carnival there are no public diversions; nor is masquerading permitted as yet. The Emperor's obsequies are to be celebrated publickly the 16th of this month; and after that, it is imagined every thing will go on in its usual course. In the mean time, to employ the minds of the populace, the Government has thought fit to bring into the city in a solemn manner, and at a great expence, a famous statue of the Virgin called the Madonna dell'Impruneta, from the place of her residence, which is upon a mountain seven miles off. It never has been practised but at times of public calamity;

and was done at present to avert the ill effects of a late great inundation, which it was feared might cause some epidemical distemper. It was introduced a fortnight ago in procession, attended by the Council of Regency, the Senate, the Nobility, and all the Religious Orders, on foot and bare-headed, and so carried to the great church, where it was frequented by an infinite concourse of people from all the country round. Among the rest I paid my devotions almost every day, and saw numbers of people possessed with the devil, who were brought to be exorcised. It was indeed in the evening, and the church-doors were always shut before the ceremonies were finished, so that I could not be eye-witness of the event; but that they were all cured is certain, for one never heard any more of them the next morning. I am to-night just returned from seeing our Lady make her exit with the same solemnities she entered. The show had a finer effect than before; for it was dark; and every body (even those of the mob that could afford it) bore a white-wax flambeau. I believe there were at least five thousand of them, and the march was near three hours in passing before the window. The subject of all this devotion is supposed to be a large Tile with a rude figure in bas-relief upon it. I say supposed, because since the time it was found (for it was found in the earth in ploughing) only two people have seen it; the one was, by good luck, a saint; the other was struck blind for his presumption. Ever since she has been covered with seven veils; nevertheless, those who approach her tabernacle cast their eyes down, for fear they should spy her through all her veils. Such is the history, as I had it from the Lady of the house where I stood to see her pass; with many other circumstances; all which she firmly believes, and ten thousand beside.

We shall go to Venice in about six weeks, or sooner. A number of German troops are upon their march into this State, in case the King of Naples thinks proper to attack it. It is certain he has asked the Pope's leave for his troops to pass through his country. The Tuscans in general are much discontented, and foolish enough to wish for a Spanish government, or any rather than this. . . .

II

April 1742—July 1756

The quarrel which interrupted Gray's grand tour with Walpole came to a head at Reggio on May 3, 1741. Leaving Walpole behind, Gray returned to London. Many years later Walpole wrote: "I am conscious that in the beginning of the differences between Gray and me, the fault was mine. I was too young, too fond of my own diversions, nay I do not doubt, too much intoxicated by indulgence, vanity, and the insolence of my situation as a Prime Minister's son, not to have been inattentive and insensible to the feelings of one I thought below me; of one whom presumption and folly perhaps made me deem not my superior *then* in parts, though I have since felt my infinite inferiority to him. I treated him insolently; he loved me and I did not think that he did."

This is surely handsome enough but it gives reason for supposing that Walpole was not at the time anything like so conciliatory. Several years were to pass before the two spoke together again. Gray returned to Cambridge in October 1742 and remained there for the rest of his life, much of the time simply taking advantage of the fact that Fellow Commoners could reside free for as long as they cared to do so. Probably the death of West, a few months earlier, provided at least another excuse for that retirement from the world which his own temperament made inevitable.

Meanwhile he was also discovering himself to be a poet. On the return journey to England he had inscribed an "Ode" in an album at the Grande Chartreuse, The "Ode to Spring" was dispatched to West the very day that his friend died, and two months later he wrote the "Ode on a Distant Prospect of Eton College." Sometime about the end of that year his mother moved to Stoke Poges and thus unconsciously created the situation which was to make possible one of the most famous poems in the English language.

In the Fall of 1745 Walpole wrote to suggest that they meet and adjust their differences. Gray hesitated, but the meeting was finally arranged and correspondence between the two began again. Though it was never to be without reserve on Gray's side, the way was prepared; it was Walpole's persistence which finally assured publication of Gray's most important poems. In the letters which follow one may read the story of Gray's scruples and strange reluctance.

To RICHARD WEST

[*c. 1 April 1742*].

I trust to the country, and that easy indolence you say you enjoy there, to restore you your health and spirits; and doubt not but, when the sun grows warm enough to tempt you from your fire-side, you will (like all other things) be the better for his influence. He is my old friend, and an excellent nurse, I assure you. Had it not been for him, life had often been to me intolerable. Pray do not imagine that Tacitus, of all authors in the world, can be tedious. An annalist, you know, is by no means master of his subject; and I think one may venture to say, that if those Pannonian affairs are tedious in his hands, in another's they would have been insupportable. However, fear not, they will soon be over, and he will make ample amends. A man, who could join the *brilliant* of wit and concise sententiousness peculiar to that age, with the truth and gravity of better times, and the deep reflection and good sense of the best moderns, cannot choose but have something to strike you. Yet what I admire in him above all this, is his detestation of tyranny, and the high spirit of liberty that every now and then breaks out, as it were, whether he would or no. I remember a sentence in his Agricola that (concise as it is) I always admired for saying much in a little compass. He speaks of Domitian, who upon seeing the last will of that General, where he had made upon him Coheir with his Wife and Daughter, 'Satis constabat lætatum eum, velut honore, judicioque: tam cæca & corrupta mens assiduis adulationibus erat, ut nesciret a bono patre non scribi hæredem, nisi malum principem'.

As to the Dunciad, it is greatly admired: the Genii of Operas and Schools, with their attendants, the pleas of the Virtuosos and Florists, and the yawns of dulness in the end, are as fine as anything he has written. The Metaphysicians' part is to me the worst; and here and there a few ill-expressed lines, and some hardly intelligible.

I take the liberty of sending you a long speech of Agrippina; much too long, but I could be glad you would retrench it. Aceronia, you may remember, had been giving quiet counsels. I fancy, if it ever be finished, it will be in the nature of Nat. Lee's Bedlam Tragedy, which had twenty-five acts and some odd scenes.

To JOHN CHUTE

[*May 24, 1742*].

My Dear Sir

Three Days ago, as I was in the Coffee-house very deep in Advertisements, a Servant came in, & waked me (as I thought) with the Name of Mr. Chute. For half a minute I was not sure, but that it was You transported into England by some strange Chance the Lord knows how; till he brought me to a Coach that seem'd to have lost it way by looking for a Needle in a Bottle of Hay, in it was a Lady, who said she was not You, but only a near relation, & was so good to give me a Letter with which I return'd to my Den in order to prey upon it. I had wrote to you but a few days ago, & am glad of so good an Excuse to do it again, which I may the better do, as my last was all out, & nothing to the Purpose, being design'd for a certain Mr. Chute at Rome, & not him at Florence.

I learn from it that I have been somewhat smarter, than I ought, but (to shew you with how little Malice) I protest I have not the least Idea what it was: my Memory would be better, did I read my own Letters so often, as I do yours. You must attribute it to a sort of kittenish Disposition, that scratches, where it means to caress; however I don't repent neither: if 'tis that, has made you write. I know, I need not ask pardon, for you have forgiven me: nay, I have a good Mind to complain myself. How could you say, that I design'd to hurt you, because I knew you could feel? I hate the thoughts of it, & would not for the world wound any thing, that was sensible. 'Tis true, I should be glad to scratch the Careless, or the Foolish, but no armour is so impenetrable, as Indifference & Stupidity, and so I may keep my Claws to myself. for another Instance of the shortness of my Memory would you believe, I have so little knowledge of the Florentine History, as not to guess, who the Lady-Errant is you mention? sure it can't be the Ricardi & her faithful Swain, or may be Mme. Gondi & the little Abbé. What you do there so long, I have no Conception. if you stay at other Places in proportion, I despair of ever seeing you again. 'Tis true indeed Mr. Mann is not every where. I am shock'd to think of his Sufferings, but he of all Men was born to suffer with a good Grace. he is a Stoick without knowing it, & seems to think Pain a Pleasure: I am very sorry to complement him upon such an Occasion, & wish with all my Heart he were not so pleased. I much fear his Books are gone already; but if not, to be sure he shall have Middleton, & the Sofa. It seems most people here are not such admirers of it, as I was: but I won't give up an inch of it for all that. did I tell you about Mr. Garrick, that the Town are horn-mad after; there are a dozen Dukes of a night at Goodmans-fields sometimes, & yet I am stiff in the opposition. our fifth Opera was the Olympiade, in which they retain'd most of Pergolesi's Songs, & yet 'tis gone already, as if it had been a poor thing of Galuppi's. two nights did I enjoy it all alone, snugg in a Nook in the Gallery, but found no one in those regions had ever heard of Pergolesi, nay, I heard several affirm it was a Composition of Pescetti's: now there is a 6th sprung up by the name of Cefalo & Procri. My Lady of Queensbury is come out against my Lady of Marlborough; & she has her

Spirit too, her Originality, but more of the Woman, I think, than t'other; as to the Facts it don't signify two pence, who's in the right; the manner of fighting, & character of the Combatants is all: 'tis hoped old Sarah will at her again. a Play of Mr. Glover's, I am told, is prepareing for the stage call'd Boadicea: it is a fine Subject, but I have not an extreme Opinion of him. the Invalides at Chelsea intend to present Ranelagh-Gardens, as a Nusance, for breaking their first Sleep with the sound of Fiddles: it opens, I think, tonight. Messieurs the Commons are to ballot for 7 Persons tomorrow, commission'd to state the publick accounts, & they are to be such, who have no places, nor are anyways dependent on the King. The Committee have petition'd for all Papers relateing to the Convention:[1] a bill has pass'd the lower House for indemnifying all, who might subject themselves to Penalties by revealing any transaction with regard to the Conduct of My Lord Orford, & tomorrow the Lords are summon'd about it. The Wit of the times consists in Satyrical Prints, I believe, there have been some Hundreds within this Month; if you have any hopeful young Designer of Caricaturas, that has a political Turn, he may pick up a pretty Subsistance here: let him pass thro' Holland to improve his Taste by the way. We are all very sorry for poor Queen Hungary; but we know of a second Battle (which perhaps you may never hear off, but from me) as how Prince Lobbycock came up in the Nick of Time, & cut 120,000 of 'em all to pieces, & how the King of Prussia narrowly scaped aboard a Ship, & so got down the Dannub to Wolf-in-Bottle, where Mr. Mallyboyce lay incamp'd, & how the Hannoverians with Prince Hissy-Castle at their head, fell upon the French Mounseers, & took him away with all his Treasure, among which is Pitt's Diamond, & the Great Cistern. All this is firmly believed here, & a vast deal more; upon the Strength of which we intend to declare War with France.

You are so obligeing as to put me in mind of our last Years

---

[1] The Convention of Madrid, signed on Jan. 14, 1739.

little expeditions; alas! Sir, they are past, & how many Years will it be, at the rate you go on, before we can possibly renew them in this Country? In all probability I shall be gone first on a long Expedition to that undiscover'd Country, from whose bourn no Traveller returns; however (if I can) I will think of you, as I sail down the *River of Eternity.* I can't help thinking, that I should find no difference almost between this world & t'other (for I converse with none but the dead here) only indeed I should receive, nor write no more Letters (for the Post is not very well regulated) if you see the King of Naples, pray talk with him on this Subject, for I see he is upon Settleing one between his country & Constantinople, & I take this to be but a little more difficult.

My Dab of Musick & Prints you are very good to think of sending with your own; to which I will add a farther Trouble by desireing you to send me some of the Roots of a certain Flower, which I have seen at Florence, it a huge white Hyacynth tinged with Pink (Mr. M. knows what I mean, by that same token that they grow sometimes in the fat Gerina's *Boosom*) I mean, if they bear a reasonable Price, which you will judge of for me: but don't give yourself any pains about it, for if they are not easily had, & at an easy Rate, I am not at all eager for them: do you talk of *strumming*? ohime! who have not seen the face of a *Haspical,*[2] since I came home; no; I have not hanged up my Harp on the Willows; however I look at my Musick now & then, that I may not forget it, for when you return, I intend to sing a Song of Thanksgiving & praise the Lord with a chearful Noise of many-stringed Instruments. Adieu! dear Sir, I am sincerely Yours

T G:

To RICHARD WEST

London, May 27, 1742.

Mine, you are to know, is a white Melancholy, or rather Leucocholy for the most part; which though it seldom laughs or

2 Harpsichord

dances, nor ever amounts to what one calls Joy or Pleasure, yet is a good easy sort of a state, and ça ne laisse que de s'amuser. The only fault of it is insipidity; which is apt now and then to give a sort of Ennui, which makes one form certain little wishes that signify nothing. But there is another sort, black indeed, which I have now and then felt, that has somewhat in it like Tertullian's rule of faith, Credo quia impossibile est; for it believes, nay, is sure of every thing that is unlikely, so it be but frightful; and, on the other hand, excludes and shuts its eyes to the most possible hopes, and every thing that is pleasurable; from this the Lord delivers us! for none but he and sunshiny weather can do it. In hopes of enjoying this kind of weather, I am going into the country for a few weeks, but shall be never the nearer any society; so, if you have any charity, you will continue to write. My life is like Harry the fourth's supper of Hens. 'Poulets a la broche, Poulets en Ragôut, Poulets en Hâchis, Poulets en Fricasées.' Reading here, Reading there; nothing but books with different sauces. Do not let me lose my desert then; for though that be Reading too, yet it has a very different flavour. The May seems to be come since your invitation; and I propose to bask in her beams and dress me in her roses. . . .

To THOMAS WHARTON

November 14, 1745.

I am not lost: here am I at Stoke, whither I came on Tuesday, & shall be again in Town on Saturday, & at Cambridge on Wednesday or Thursday. You may be curious to know what has past. I wrote a Note the Night I came, & immediately received a very civil Answer. I went the following Evening to see *the Party* (as Mrs. Foible says) was something abash'd at his Confidence: he came to meet me, kiss'd me on both Sides with all the Ease of one, who receives an Acquaintance just come out of the Country, squatted me into a Fauteuil, begun to talk of the Town & this & that & t'other, & continued with little Interruption for three Hours, when I took my Leave very indifferently pleased, but treated with wondrous Good-breeding. I supped with him next night (as he desired) Ashton was there, whose Formalities tickled me inwardly, for he I found was to be angry about the Letter I had wrote him. However in going home together our Hackney-Coach jumbled us into a Sort of Reconciliation: he hammer'd out somewhat like an Excuse; & I received it very readily, because I cared not two pence, whither it were true or not. So we grew the best Acquaintance imaginable, & I set with him on Sunday some Hours alone, when he inform'd me of abundance of Anecdotes much to my Satisfaction, & in short open'd (I really believe) his Heart to me with that Sincerity, that I found I had still less Reason to have a good Opinion of him, than (if possible) I ever had before. Next Morning I breakfasted alone with Mr. W. when we had all the Eclaircissement I ever expected, & I left him far better satisfied than I had been hitherto. When I return, I shall see him again. Such is the Epitome of my four Days. Mr. & Mrs. Simms & Mlle. Nanny have done the Honours of Leaden Hall to a Miracle, & all joyn in a Compliment to the Doctor. Your Brother is well, the Books are in good Condition. Mme. Chenevix has frightened me with Ecritoires she asks three Guinea's for, that are not worth three half pence: I have been in several Shops & found nothing pretty. I fear it must be bespoke at last.

the Day after I went you received a little Letter directed to me, that seems wrote with a Skewer. Please to open it, & you'll find a receipt of Dan. Adcock for ten Pound, which I will beg you to receive of Gillham for me. If the Letter miscarried, pray take care the Money is paid to no one else. I expect to have a Letter from you when I come to Town, at your Lodgeings. . . . Adieu, Sir, I am sincerely Yours

T G:

To THOMAS WHARTON

[*8 Oct. 1746*].

My Dear Wharton,

This is only to entreat you would order mes Gens to clean out the Appartments, spread the Carpets, air the Beds, put up the Tapestry, unpaper the Frames, &c. fit to receive a great Potentate, that comes down in the Flying Coach drawn by Green Dragons on Friday the 10th Instant. As the Ways are bad, & the Dragons a little out of Repair (for they don't actually fly; but only go, like a lame Ostrich, something between a Hop & a Trot) it will probably be late when he lands, so he would not chuse to be known, & desires there may be no Bells, nor Bonfires: but as Persons incog. love to be seen, he will slip into the Coffee House. Is Mr. Trollope among you? Good lack! he will pull off my Head for never writeing to him. Oh Conscience! Conscience!

To HORACE WALPOLE

Cambridge [*c. Feb. 22*], *1747*.

As one ought to be particularly careful to avoid blunders in a compliment of condolence, it would be a sensible satisfaction to me (before I testify my sorrow, and the sincere part I take in your misfortune) to know for certain, who it is I lament. I knew Zara and Selima, (Selima, was it? or Fatima) or rather I knew them both together; for I cannot justly say which was which. Then as to your handsome Cat, the name you distinguish her by, I am no less at a loss, as well knowing one's handsome cat is always the cat one likes best; or, if one be alive and the other dead, it is usually the latter that is the handsomest. Besides, if the point were never so clear, I hope you do not think me so ill-bred or so imprudent as to forfeit all my interest in the surviver: Oh no! I would rather seem to mistake, and imagine to be sure it must be the tabby one that had met with this sad accident. Till this affair is a little better determined, you will excuse me if I do not begin to cry:

'Tempus inane peto, requiem, spatiumque doloris.'

Which interval is the more convenient, as it gives time to rejoice with you on your new honors. This is only a beginning; I reckon next week we shall hear you are a Free-Mason, or a Gormogon[1] at least.

To JOHN CHUTE

[*c. 1748?*].

My Dear Sir

I was yesterday told, that Turner (the Professor of Modern History here) was dead in London. If it be true; I conclude, it is now too late to begin asking for it: but we had (if you remember) some Conversation on that Head at Twickenham; & as you have probably found some Opportunity to mention it to Mr. W. since, I would gladly know his Thoughts about it. What he can do, he only can tell us: what he will do, if he can, is with me no Question. If he could find a proper Channel; I certainly might ask it with as much, or more Propriety, than any one in this Place. If any thing were done, it should be as private as possible; for if the People, who have any Sway here, could prevent it, I think they would most zealously. I am not sorry for writing you a little interested Letter: perhaps it is a Stratagem: the only one I had left, to provoke an Answer from you, & revive our—Correspondence, shall I call it? There are many particulars relating to you, that have long interested me more than twenty Matters of this Sort, but you have had no Regard for my Curiosity: and yet it is something, that deserves a better Name! I don't so much as know your Direction, or that of Mr. Whithed. Adieu! I am ever

Yours
T Gray

---

[1] A member of a society imitating the Freemasons, founded early in the eighteenth century.

To HORACE WALPOLE

[*Cambridge, Feb. 11, 1751*].

My Dear Sir

As you have brought me into a little Sort of Distress, you must assist me, I believe, to get out of it, as well as I can. Yesterday I had the Misfortune of receiving a Letter from certain Gentlemen (as their Bookseller expresses it) who have taken the *Magazine of Magazines* into their Hands. They tell me, that an *ingenious* Poem, call'd, *Reflections* in a Country-Churchyard, has been communicated to them, which they are printing forthwith: that they are inform'd, that the *excellent* Author of it is I by name, & that they beg not only his *Indulgence,* but the *Honor of his Correspondence,* &c. as I am not at all disposed to be either so indulgent, or so correspondent, as they desire; I have but one bad Way left to escape the Honour they would inflict upon me. & therefore am obliged to desire you would make Dodsley print it immediately (which may be done in less than a Week's time) from your Copy, but without my Name, in what Form is most convenient for him, but in his best Paper & Character. He must correct the Press himself, & print it without any Interval between the Stanza's, because the Sense is in some Places continued beyond them; & the Title must be, Elegy, wrote in a Country Church-yard. If he would add a Line or two to say it came into his Hands by Accident, I should like it better. If you think fit, the 102d Line may be read

Awake, & faithful to her wonted Fires.

but if this be worse than before; it must go, as it was. in the 126th, for *ancient* Thorn, read *aged.*

If you behold the Mag. of Mag.'s in the Light that I do, you will not refuse to give yourself this Trouble on my Account, which you have taken of your own Accord before now. Adieu, Sir, I am

Yours ever

T G:

If Dodsley don't do this immediately, he may as well let it alone.

To HORACE WALPOLE

Ash-Wednesday [*Feb. 20*], *Cambridge, 1751.*

My dear Sir,

You have indeed conducted with great decency my little *misfortune:* you have taken a paternal care of it, and expressed much more kindness than could have been expected from so near a relation. But we are all frail; and I hope to do as much for you another time. Nurse Dodsley has given it a pinch or two in the cradle, that (I doubt) it will bear the marks of as long as it lives. But no matter: we have ourselves suffered under her hands before now; and besides, it will only look the more careless, and by *accident* as it were. I thank you for your advertisement, which saves my honour, and in a manner *bien flatteuse pour moi,* who should be put to it even to make myself a compliment in good English.

You will take me for a mere poet, and a fetcher and carrier of singsong, if I tell you that I intend to send you the beginning of a drama, not mine, thank God, as you'll believe, when you hear it is finished, but wrote by a person whom I have a very good opinion of. It is (unfortunately) in the manner of the ancient drama, with choruses, which I am, to my shame, the occasion of; for, as great part of it was at first written in that form, I would not suffer him to change it to a play fit for the stage, as he intended, because the lyric parts are the best of it, and they must have been lost. The story is Saxon, and the language has a tang of Shakespeare, that suits an old-fashioned fable very well. In short, I don't do it merely to amuse you, but for the sake of the author, who wants a judge, and so I would lend him *mine:* yet not without your leave, lest you should have us up to dirty our stockings at the bar of your house for wasting the time and politics of the *nation.* Adieu, sir!

I am ever yours,

T. Gray.

To HORACE WALPOLE

Wednesday—[*July 8, 1752*] *Stoke.*

I am at present at Stoke, to which I came at half an Hour's Warning upon the News I received of my Mother's Illness, & did not expect to have found her alive: but as I found her much better, & she continues so, I shall be very glad to make you a Visit at Strawberry, whenever you give me Notice of a convenient time. I am surprized at the Print, which far surpasses my Idea of London Graving. The Drawing itself was so finished, that I suppose, it did not require all the Art I had imagined to copy it tolerably. My Aunts, just now, seeing me open your Letter, take it to be a Burying-Ticket enclosed, & ask, whether any body has left me a Ring? And so they still conceive it to be, even with all their Spectacles on. Heaven forbid they should suspect it to belong to any Verses of mine; they would burn me for a Poet. Mr. Bentley (I believe) will catch a better Idea of Stoke-House from any old Barn he sees, than from my Sketch: but I will try my Skill. I forbid no Banes; but am satisfied, if your Design succeed so well as you intend it. And yet I know, it will be accompanied with something not at all agreeable to me. Adieu! I am

Yours ever

T G.

To ROBERT DODSLEY

Feb. 12. Cambridge [*1753*].

Sir

I am not at all satisfied with the Title. To have it conceived, that I publish a Collection of *Poems* (half a dozen little Matters, four of which too have already been printed again & again) thus pompously adorned would make me appear very highly ridiculous. I desire it may be understood (which is the truth) that the Verses are only subordinate, & explanatory to the Drawings, & suffer'd by me to come out thus only for that reason. Therefore if you yourself prefix'd this Title, I desire it may be alter'd; or if Mr. W. order'd it so, that you would tell him, why I wish it were changed in the manner I mention'd to you at first, or to that purpose: for the more I consider it, the less I can bear it, as it now stands. I even think, there is an uncommon sort of Simplicity, that looks like affectation, in putting our plain Christian and Surnames without a Mr. before them; but this (if it signifies any thing) I easily give up; the other I can not. You need not apprehend, that this Change in the Title will be any prejudice to the Sale of the book. A showy title-page may serve to sell a Pamphlet of a shilling or two; but this is not of a price for chance-customers, whose eye is caught in passing by a window; & could never sell but from the notion the Town may entertain of the Merit of the Drawings, which they will be instructed in by some, that understand such things.

I thank you for the Offer you make me, but I shall be contented with three Copies, two of which you will send me, & keep the third, till I acquaint you where to send it. If you will let me know the exact day they will come out a little time beforehand, I will give you a direction. You will remember to send two copies to Dr. Thomas Wharton, M.D. at Durham. Perhaps you may have burnt my Letters, so I will again put down the Title

Designs by Mr. R. Bentley
for six Poems of
Mr. T. Gray.

I am, Sir, Your humble Servant
T G:

To HORACE WALPOLE

Cambridge. Feb. 13. 1753.

Sure You are not out of your Wits! this I know, if you suffer my Head to be printed, you infallibly will put me out of mine. I conjure you immediately to put a stop to any such design. Who is at the Expence of engraving it, I know not; but if it be Dodsley, I will make up the Loss to him. The thing, as it was, I know will make me ridiculous enough; but to appear in proper Person at the head of my works, consisting of half a dozen Ballads in 30 Pages, would be worse than the Pillory. I do assure you, if I had received such a Book with such a frontispice without any warning, I believe, it would have given me a Palsy. Therefore I rejoice to have received this Notice; & shall not be easy, till you tell me all thoughts of it are laid aside. I am extremely in earnest, & can't bear even the Idea!

I had wrote to Dodsley to tell him, how little I liked the Title he had prefix'd, but your letter has put all that out of my Head. If you think it necessary to print these Explanations for the use of People that have no eyes, I could be glad, they were a little alter'd. I am to my shame in your debt for a long letter, but I can not think of anything else, till you have set me at ease. Adieu, I am

Yours ever,

T G:

To HORACE WALPOLE

Stoke. Feb. 27 [*1753*].

I am obliged on the sudden to come hither to see my poor mother who is in a condition between Life & Death, tho' (I think) much nearer the latter. Yet I could not help telling you, I had received your Letter, & am pleased to find, I was in the wrong. you may be sure, I was not willing to think you so. Do what you please about the title, if it is time; but it seems to me the less of Puff or Ostentation it has, the better it will be, even for Dodsley. Excuse my brevity, Adieu, I am ever

Yours

T G:

To THOMAS WHARTON

March 15 [*1753*]—*Stoke.*

My dear Wharton

I judge by this time you are in town. The reason that I thought would have deprived me of the pleasure of seeing you is now at an end. My poor Mother, after a long & painful Struggle for life, expired on Sunday morning. When I have seen her buried, I shall come to London, & it will be a particular satisfaction to me to find you there. If you can procure me a tolerable lodging near you, be so good (if you can conveniently) to let me know the night you receive this; if not, I shall go to my old Landlord in Jermyn Street. I believe, I shall come on Tuesday, & stay a few days, for I must return hither to pay my Aunt her Arrears, which she will demand with great Exactness. Adieu, dear Sir, I am

Ever yours,

T Gray.

To THOMAS WHARTON

Stoke, Sept. 18. 1754.

Dear Sir

I rejoice to find you at last settled to your heart's content, & delight to hear you talk of *giving your house some Gothic ornaments* already. If you project any thing, I hope it will be entirely within doors; & don't let me (when I come gaping into Coleman-street) be directed to the Gentleman's at the ten Pinnacles, or with the Church-porch at his door. I am glad you enter into the Spirit of Strawberry-Castle. It has a purity & propriety of Gothicism in it (with very few exceptions,) that I have not seen elsewhere. The eating-room & library were not compleated, when I was there, & I want to know, what effect they have. My Lord Radnor's Vagaries (I see) did not keep you from doing justice to his situation, which far surpasses every thing near it, & I do not know a more *laughing* Scene, than that about Twickenham & Richmond. Dr. Akenside (I perceive) is no Conjurer in Architecture, especially when he talks of the Ruins of Persepolis, which are no more Gothic, than they are Chinese. the Egyptian Style (see Dr. Pococke, not his discourses, but his prints) was apparently the Mother of ye Greek; & there is such a similitude between the Egyptian, & those Persian Ruins, as gave room to Diodorus to affirm, that the old buildings of Persia were certainly perform'd by Egyptian Artists. as to the other part of his opinion, that the

Gothic manner is the Saracen or Moorish, he has a great Authority to support him, that of Sr. Christopher Wren, & yet (I can not help thinking) is undoubtedly wrong. The Palaces in Spain I never saw but in description, which gives us little or no Idea of things; but the Doge's Palace at Venice I have seen (which is in the Arabesque manner) & the houses of Barbary you may see in Dr. Shaw's book, not to mention abundance of other eastern Buildings in Turkey, Persia, &c. that we have views of, & they seem plainly to be corruptions of the Greek Architecture, broke into little parts indeed, & cover'd with little ornaments, but in a taste very distinguishable from that we call Gothic. There is one thing, that runs thro' the Moorish Buildings, that an Imitator would certainly have been first struck with, & would have tried to copy, & that is the Cupola's, which cover everything, Baths, Apar[t]ments, & even Kitchens. Yet who ever saw a Gothic Cupola? It is a thing plainly of Greek original. I do not see any thing but the slender Spires, that serve for steeples, which may perhaps be borrowed from the Saracen Minarets on their Mosques.

I was in Northamptonshire, when I received your Letter, but am now returned hither. I have been at Warwick, which is a place worth seeing. The Town is on an eminence surrounded every way with a fine cultivated Valley, thro' which the Avon winds, & at the distance of 5 or 6 miles, a circle of hills well wooded, & with various objects crowning them, that close the Prospect. Out of the town on one side of it rises a rock, that might remind one of your rocks at Durham, but that it is not so savage, or so lofty, & that the river, which washes its foot, is perfectly clear, & so gentle, that its current is hardly visible. Upon it stands the Castle, the noble old residence of the Beauchamps & Neville's, & now of Earl Brooke. He has sash'd the great Appartment, that's to be sure, (I can't help these things) & being since told, that square sash-windows were not Gothic, he has put certain whim-wams withinside the glass, which appearing through are to look like fretwork. Then he has scooped out a little Burrough in the mass walls of the place for his little self & his children, which is hung with Paper & printed Linnen, & carved chimney-pieces, in the exact manner of Berkley-square or Argyle-Buildings. what in short can a Lord do now a days, that is lost in a great old solitary Castle, but sculk about, & get into the first hole he finds, as a Rat would do in like case. A pretty long old stone-bridge leads you into the town with a Mill at the end of it, over which the rock rises with the Castle upon it with all its battlements & queer ruin'd towers, & on your left hand the Avon strays thro' the Park, whose ancient Elms seem to remember Sir Philip Sidney, (who often walk'd under them) and talk of him to this day. The Beauchamp Earls of Warwick lie under stately Monuments in the Choir of the great Church, & in our Lady's Chappel adjoining to it. There also lie Ambrose Dudley, E. of Warwick; & his Brother, the famous Lord Leicester, with Lettice, his Countess. This Chappel is preserved entire, tho' the Body of the Church was burnt down 60 years ago, & rebuilt by Sir C. Wren. I had heard often of Guy-Cliff two miles from the town, so I walked to see it; & of all improvers commend me to Mr. Greathead, its present Owner. He shew'd it me himself, & is literally a fat young Man with a head & face much bigger than they are usually worn. It was naturally a very agreeable rock, whose Cliffs cover'd with large trees hung beetleing over the Avon, which twists twenty ways in sight of it. There was the Cell of Guy, Earl of Warwick, cut in the living stone, where he died a Hermit (as you may see in a penny History, that hangs upon the rails in Moorfields) there were his fountains bubbling out of the Cliff; there was a Chantry founded to his memory in Henry the 6th's time. But behold the Trees are cut down to make room for flowering shrubs, the rock is cut up, till it is as smooth & as sleek as sattin; the river has a gravel-walk by its side; the Cell is a Grotta with cockle-shells and looking-glass; the fountains have an iron-gate before them, and the Chantry is a Barn, or a little House. Even the poorest bits of nature, that remain, are daily threatned, for he says (& I am sure, when the Greatheads are once set upon a thing, they will do it) he is determined, it shall be *all new*. These were his words, & they are Fate. I have also been at Stow, at Woburn (the Du[ke] of Bedford's), and at Wroxton (Lord Guilford's) but I defer these Chapt[ers] till we meet. I shall only tell you for your Comfort, that th[e] part of Northamptonshire, where I may have been, is in fruits, in flowers [& in] corn very near a fortnight behind this part of Buckinghamshire, that they have no nightingales, & that the other birds are almost as silent, as at Durham. It is rich land, but upon a Clay, & in a very bleak, high, exposed situation. I hope, you have had some warm weather, since you last complained of the South. I have thoughts of seeing you about Michaelmas, tho' I shall not stay long in town. I should have been at Cambridge before now, if the D. of Newcastle & his foundation-stone would have let me, but I want them to have done before I go. I am sorry Mr. Brown should be the only one, that has stood upon Punctilio's with me, & would not write first. Pray tell him so. Mason is (I believe) in town, or at Chiswick. [no news of Tuthill]: I wrote a long letter to him in answer to one he wrote me, but no reply. Adieu, I am ever Yrs,

T G.

Brown call'd here this morning, before I was up, & breakfasted with me.

To THOMAS WHARTON

Aug. 21. 1755. Stoke.

Dear Doctor

Instead of going to Twickenham I was obliged to send my excuses, & the same day Mr. W. sent a messenger to say he was confined in Town with a Fever & a Rash. He has since wrote me word, that he is well again; but for me I continue much as I was, & have been but once out of the house to walk, since I return'd from Hampshire. Being much inclined to bleeding myself, I yet was fearful to venture, least it should bring on a regular fit of the Gout, so I sent for advice at last, & expected Dr. Hayes should call me presently, whether it were Gout or Rheumatism. In his talk he treated it rather as the former, but his prescription appears to me to be meant for the latter. You will judge. He took away 10 or 11 *Oz* of blood, & order'd these draughts night & morning:—*Sal: Absinth. Succ: Limon. finitâ effervescentiâ add: Aqu: Alexit. Simpl:, Menth: Piperit, Magnes. alb., Tinct: G. Guiac. Spirituos.* The quantities I can't read; only I think there is a Dram of the Tincture, & ½ a Dram of Magnesia in each draught. The Blood had no sign of inflammation, but of a bright red: the Serum of a dark yellow with little transparency, not viscid to the touch. The draughts (which I took over night only) made me sweat almost immediately, & open'd a little in the morning. The consequence is, that I have still many slight complaints. Broken & unrefreshing sleeps, as before. Less feverish than I was, in a morning: instead of it a sensation of weariness and soreness in both feet, which goes off in the day. A frequent dizziness & lightness of head. easily fatigued with motion. Sometimes a little pain in my breast, as I had in the winter. These symptoms are all too slight to make an illness; but they do not make perfect health. That is sure.

Tho' I allow abundance for your kindness & partiality to me, I am yet much pleased with the good opinion you seem to have of the *Bard*. you may alter that *Robed in the Sable,* &c, almost in your own words, thus

With fury pale, & pale with woe,
Secure of fate, the Poet stood &c.

Tho' *haggard,* which conveys to you the Idea of a *Witch,* is indeed only a metaphor taken from an unreclaim'd Hawk, which is call'd a *Haggard,* & looks wild & *farouche* & jealous of its liberty. I have sent now Stohewer a bit more of the *prophecy,* & desire him to shew it you immediately: it is very rough & unpolish'd at present. Adieu, dear Sir, I am ever

Truly Yours
T G.

To WILLIAM MASON

Dear Mason

I feel a contrition for my long silence; & yet perhaps it is the last thing you trouble your head about. Nevertheless I will be as sorry, as if you took it ill. I am sorry too to see you so punctilious, as to stand upon answers, & never to come near me, till I have regularly left my name at your door, like a Mercer's Wife, that imitates People, who go a-visiting. I would forgive you this, if you could possibly suspect I were doing any thing, that I liked better. for then your formality might look like being piqued at my negligence; which has somewhat in it like kindness: but you know I am at Stoke, hearing, seeing, doing, absolutely nothing. Not such a nothing, as you do at Tunbridge, chequer'd & diversified with a succession of fleeting colours; but heavy, lifeless, without form, & void; sometimes almost as black, as the *Moral* of Voltaire's Lisbon, which angers you so. I have had no more pores & muscular inflations, & am only troubled with this depression of mind. You will not expect therefore I should give you any account of my *Verve,* which is at best (you know) of so delicate a constitution, & has such weak nerves, as not to stir out of its chamber above three days in a year. But I shall enquire after yours, & why it is off again? It has certainly worse nerves than mine, if your Reviewers have frighted it. Sure I (not to mention a score of your Uncles and Aunts) am something a better Judge, than all the Man-Midwives & Presbyterian Parsons, that ever were born. Pray give me leave to ask you. do you find yourself tickled with the commendations of such Peoples? (for you have your share of these too) I dare say not. Your Vanity has certainly a better taste. and can then the censure of such Criticks move you? I own, it is an impertinence in these Gentry to talk of one at all either in good or in bad, but this we must all swallow, I mean not only we, that write, but all the *we's* that ever did any thing to be talk'd of. I canot pretend to be learned without books, nor to know the Druids from the Pelasgi at this distance from Cambridge, I can only tell you not to go & take the Mona for the Isle of Man. It it Anglesey, a tract of plain country, very fertile, but picturesque only from the view it has of Caernarvonshire, from which it is separated by the Menai, a narrow arm of the Sea. Forgive me for supposing in you such a want of erudition.

I congratulate you on our glorious successes in the Mediterranean. shall we go in time, & hire a house together in Switzerland? It is a fine poetical country to look at, & no body there will understand a word we say or write. Pray, let me know what you are about, what new acquaintances you have made at Tunbridge, how you do in body & in mind? Believe me ever sincerely

Yours

T G:

Stoke—July, 23. 1756

Have you read Mme. Maintenon's Letters. When I saw Lord John in Town, he said if his Brother went to Ireland, you were to go *second* Chaplain. But it seem'd to me not at all certain, that the Duke would return thither. You probably know by this time.

III

September 1756—June 1771

A little more than three weeks before Dodsley published Gray's *Six Poems* with decorations by Bentley, the poet's mother had died. He was still to publish several poems—notably the "Progress of Poetry," "The Bard," and "The Descent of Odin"—which are highly esteemed by critics and historians but none of which has ever enjoyed the popularity of either the "Elegy" or the "Ode on a Distant Prospect of Eton College."

By now the pattern of Gray's life was fixed beyond the possibility of change. He still left the university occasionally for journeys or to stay in the country. He saw friends from time to time, and of course he continued his correspondence with Walpole and with others. But he was more and more absorbed in his curious antiquarian and other researches, which seem never to have been intended for any public use. And he resisted all efforts to draw him into a more active life. He declined the offer of a secretaryship to the Earl of Bristol at Lisbon and, somewhat more surprisingly, in 1757, the office of Poet Laureate. In his own mind the most important event to take place about this time was probably his removal in a huff from Pembroke College to Peterhouse when the authorities of the former refused to take with sufficient seriousness the prank of a group of undergraduates who knew of his phobia and, early one morning, shouted "Fire!" outside his window in the disappointed hope of seeing the poet clamber down a ladder he had provided for that purpose.

There is some reason for believing that Gray's later years were somewhat less melancholy and tormented than the earlier ones had been. He inherited money from his aunt in 1758; he spent more of his time wandering about inspecting ancient buildings; and for two years he maintained lodgings in London and he read at the British Museum. Undoubtedly the appointment as Regius Professor of Modern History gratified him—especially in view of the fact that it entailed no duties.

Almost exactly three years after assuming the professorship Gray died calmly after a somewhat painful illness. For whatever strange reasons, life had never seemed to him very much of a boon, and not long before the end he turned to a cousin who was seated by his bedside to say quietly, "Molly, I shall die."

To HORACE WALPOLE

Sept. 8, 1756. the Vine.

Poor Mr. Chute has now had the Gout for these five days with such a degree of pain & uneasiness, as he never felt before. Whether to attribute it to Dr. La Cour's forcing medecines, or to a little cold he got as soon as he came hither, I know not, but for above forty hours it seem'd past all human suffering, & he lay screaming like a Man upon the rack. The torture was so great, that (against my judgement & even his own) he was forced to have recourse to [an] infusion of Poppy-heads, which Cocchi used to give him, & in [half] an hours time was easy, fell into a gentle perspiration, [&] slept many hours. This was the night before last, & all yesterday he continued chearful & in spirits. At night (as he expected) the pain returned, not so violent, but in more places, for now it is in one foot, both knees, & one hand, and I hourly dread it will increase again to its former rage. If any thing sudden happen, who can I send to? Here is no assistance nearer than a Dr. Langrish at Winchester, of whom he has no great opinion. as to Lacour he is enraged against him, & looks upon him as the cause of all he suffers. I can not think there is any danger, for tho' with all this he is at times in a high Fever, yet it seems to depend upon the Gout entirely, increasing & abating with the pain. But if anything unexpected happen, here are no body but myself & Muntz in the house, would you advise to send to Mrs. Pawlet, or to whom? You will oblige me, if you will answer me in a loose paper, for he must see your Letter. It will be a charity too to insert any thing of news, or whatever you please to tell us, for when he gets any respite from pain, he is capable & desirous of entertainment, & talks with an eagerness of spirits, that seems to make part of his distemper. Pray tell us how Mr. Man does. I am ever

Yours

T G:

To HORACE WALPOLE

The Vine. Sept. [*12*]. *Sunday.* [*1756*].

I have the pleasure to tell you that after repeating once again his infusion of Poppies, which caused each time an entire cessation from pain, & an easy perspiration for near 24 hours, Mr. Chute has had no return of his tortures, but for these four days has continued in a very tolerable state, chearful enough & in good spirits in the day-time, his appetite beginning to return, & all last night pass'd in quiet & natural sleep. But he is (as you may imagine) still nail'd to his bed, & much weaken'd. God knows, when he will be able to get up, or bear any motion, & the least cold, as Autumn is coming on, will certainly bring it all back again. I am quite of your opinion about going to Town, as soon as it is possible; & had of my own accord talk'd about it, but he seems rather set against it: however I hope to prevail. As to the Tracies, I think he told me just before this illness, that they were all coming, & he had wrote to hinder it on some pretence or other. what you say about Mrs. P. is very true. I only mention'd her, because she was more within reach than any body else: but I have now no farther thought of danger.

We are much obliged to you for your News, & hope, when you have leisure, again to hear from you. I am

Yours ever

T G:

To HORACE WALPOLE

Stoke, July 11, 1757.

I will not give you the trouble of sending your chaise for me. I intend to be with you on Wednesday in the evening. If the press stands still all this time for me, to be sure it is dead in child-bed.

I do not love notes, though you see I had resolved to put two or three. They are signs of weakness and obscurity. If a thing cannot be understood without them, it had better be not understood at all. If you will be vulgar, and pronounce it *Lunnun,* instead of London, I can't help it. Caradoc I have private reasons against; and besides it is in reality Carādoc, and will not stand in the verse.

I rejoice you can fill all your *vuides.* the Maintenon could not, and that was her great misfortune. Seriously though, I congratulate you on your happiness, and seem to understand it. The receipt is obvious: it is only, Have something to do; but how few can apply it!—Adieu!

I am ever yours,

T. Gray

To HORACE WALPOLE

Stoke. Aug. 10, 1757.

I am extremely sorry to hear of poor Mr. Bentley's illness. What I can not account for is, that You or He should trust such a Dog of an Apothecary, after he had shew'd himself, to do any thing, even to sell medecines; when it is just as easy for him to put in a grain of slow poison, as to administer a dose of pure & innocent brown-Paper.

Dodsley sent me some copies[1] last week: they are very pleasant to the eye, & will do no dishonor to your Press. As you are but young in the trade, you will excuse me if I tell you, that some little inaccuracies have escaped your eye, as in the 9th page

---

[1] Of the Strawberry Hill edition of the two odes, which had been published by Dodsley.

Lab'rinth's & *Echo's,* (which are Nominatives plural,) with Apostrophes after them, as tho' they were Genitives singular; & P. 16, sorrow & solitude without capital letters. Besides certain Commas here & there omitted. If you do not commit greater faults in your next work, I shall grow jealous of Hentzerus.

I am going to add to the trouble I have given you by desiring you would tell me, what you hear any body say, (I mean, if any body says any thing). I know you will forgive this vanity of an Author, as the vanity of a Printer is a little interested in the same cause. The Garricks have been here for three days much to my entertainment. If you see him, do not fail to make him tell you the story of *Bull & Poker*. Adieu, I am ever

Yours

T G:

To THOMAS WHARTON

Aug. 17. 1757. Stoke.

Dear Doctor

It feels to me as if it were a long while, since I heard from you. Not a word to flatter or to abash the vanity of an Author! Suffer me then to tell you, that I hear, we are not at all popular. The great objection is obscurity, no body knows what we would be at. One Man (a Peer) I have been told of, that thinks the last Stanza of the 2d Ode relates to Charles the first & Oliver Cromwell. In short the Συνετοί appear to be still fewer, than even I expected.

You will imagine all this does not go very deep; but I have been almost eversince I was here exceedingly dispirited, besides being really ill in body. No gout, but something feverish, that seems to come almost every morning, & disperses soon after I am up. The Cobhams are here, & as civil as usual. Garrick & his Wife have been down with them some days, & are soon to come again. except the little amusement they give me, & two volumes of the Encyclopedie now almost exhausted, I have nothing but my own thoughts to feed upon, & you know they are of the gloomy cast. Write to me then for *sweet St. Charity,* & remember, that while I am my own, I am most faithfully

Yours

T G:

To HORACE WALPOLE

Stoke. Oct. 13. 1757.

It will be three weeks or more before I can come to Town. I have had, almost eversince I was here, a much worse state of health than I have been used to, & particularly of late: they advise me to force a fit of the Gout, but methinks it is better to bear with a number of lesser maladies. I am not however at present confined by them, & therefore leave you to weigh my infirmities against your own impatience. If it won't stay, till I see you in London, & you will hazard the sending your chaise on Wednesday next, to be sure I will come, if I am able.

I begin at this distance with telling you, that tho' I admire rapidity in writing, & perseverance in finishing, being two talents that I want; yet I do not admire rapidity in *printing,* because this is a thing, that I or any body, can do. I am

Yours ever

T G:

To WILLIAM MASON

Dec. 19. 1757.

Dear Mason

Tho' I very well know the bland emollient saponaceous qualities both of Sack & Silver,[1] yet if any great Man would say to me, 'I make you *Rat-Catcher* to his Majesty with a salary of 300£ a-year & two Butts of the best Malaga; and tho' it has been usual to catch a mouse or two (for form's sake) in publick once a year, yet to You, Sir, we shall not stand upon these things'. I can not say, I should jump at it. Nay, if they would drop the very name of the

[1] The reference is to the post of Poet Laureate, part of whose emolument consisted formerly of an allowance of Canary wine or sack.

Office, & call me *Sinecure* to the King's majesty I should still feel a little awkward, & think every body, I saw, smelt a Rat about me: but I do not pretend to blame any one else, that has not the same sensations. for my part I would rather be Serjeant-Trumpeter, or Pin-Maker to the Palace. Nevertheless I interest myself a little in the History of it, & rather wish somebody may accept it, that will retrieve the credit of the thing, if it be retrievable, or ever had any credit. Rowe was, I think, the last Man of character that had it. As to Settle, whom you mention, he belong'd to my Lord Mayor, not to the King. Eusden was a Person of great hopes in his youth, tho' at last he turned out a drunken Parson. Dryden was as disgraceful to the Office from his character, as the poorest Scribler could have been from his verses. [In sh]ort the office itself has always humbled the Pos[sess]or hitherto (even in an age, when Kings were somebody) if he were a poor Writer by making him more conspicuous, and if he were a good one, by setting him at war with the little fry of his own profession, for there are poets little enough to envy even a Poet-Laureat.

I am obliged to you for your news, pray send me some more, & better of the sort. I can tell you nothing in return, so your generosity will be the greater. Only Dick is going to give up his rooms, & live at Ashwell. Mr. Treasurer sets Sir Mathew Lambe at naught, & says, he has sent him reasons half a sheet at a time; & Mr. Brown attests his veracity, as an eye-witness. I have had nine pages of criticism on the Bard sent me in an anonymous letter, directed to the *Rev.* Mr. G. at Strawberry-Hill, & if I have a mind to hear as much more on the other Ode, I am told, where I may direct. he seems a good sensible Man, & I dare say, a Clergyman. He is very frank, & indeed much ruder, than he means to be. Adieu, Dear Mason, & believe, that I am too.

To THOMAS WHARTON

Feb. 21. 1758.

Dear Doctor

I feel very ungrateful (which is the most uneasy of all feelings) in that I have never once enquired, how you and your family enjoy the region of air & sunshine, into which you are removed, & with what contempt you look back on the perpetual fogs, that hang over Mrs. Payne & Mrs. Paterson. Yet you certainly have not been the less in my mind: that at least has pack'd up with you, has help'd Mrs. Wharton to arrange the mantle-piece, & drank tea *next summer* in the Grotto. But I am much puzzled about the Bishop & his fixtures, & do not stomach the loss of that money.

Would you know, what I am doing? I doubt, you have been told already, & hold my employment cheap enough: but every one must judge of his own *capabilities,* & *cut* his amusements according to his disposition. The drift of my present studies is to know, wherever I am, what lies within reach, that may be worth seeing. whether it be Building, ruin, park, garden, prospect, picture, or monument; to whom it does, or has belong'd, & what has been the characteristick, & taste of different ages. You will say, this is the object of all Antiquaries, but pray, what Antiquary ever saw these objects in the same light, or desired to know them for a like reason? In short say what you please, I am persuaded, whenever my list is finish'd, you will approve it, & think it of no small use. My spirits are very near the *freezing point,* & for some hours of the day this exercise by its warmth & gentle motion serves to raise them a few degrees higher. I hope the misfortune, that has befall'n Mrs. Cibber's Canary-bird will not be the ruin of *Agis.* It is probable you will have curiosity enough to see it, as it comes from the Writer of Douglas: I expect your opinion. I am told, that Swift's History of the Tory-Administration is in the Press, & that Stuart's Attica will be out this spring. Adieu, Dear Sir, I am ever

Yours

T G:

Mr. Brown joins his compliments with mine to you & Mrs. Wharton.

To THOMAS WHARTON

Cambridge, March 8, 1758.

It is indeed for want of spirits, as you suspect, that my studies lie among the Cathedrals, and the Tombs, and the Ruins. To think, though to little purpose, has been the chief amusement of my days; and when I would not, or cannot think, I dream. At present I find myself able to write a Catalogue, or to read the Peerage book, or Miller's Gardening Dictionary, and am thankful that there are such employments and such authors in the world. Some people, who hold me cheap for this, are doing perhaps what is not half so well worth while. As to posterity, I may ask, (with some body whom I have forgot) what has it ever done to oblige me?

To make a transition from myself to as poor a subject, the Tragedy of Agis; I cry to think that it should be by the Author of Douglas: Why, it is all modern Greek; the story is an antique statue painted white and red, frized, and dressed in a negligée made by a Yorkshire mantua-maker. Then here is the Miscellany (Mr. Dodsley has sent me the whole set gilt and lettered, I thank him). Why, the two last volumes are worse than the four first; particularly Dr. Akenside is in a deplorable way. What signifies Learning and the Antients, (Mason will say triumphantly) why should people read Greek to lose their imagination, their ear, and their mother tongue? But then there is Mr. Shenstone, who trusts to nature and simple sentiment, why does he do no better? he goes hopping along his own gravel-walks, and never deviates from the beaten paths for fear of being lost.

I have read Dr. Swift, and am disappointed. There is nothing of the negotiations that I have not seen better in M. de Torcy before. The manner is careless, and has little to distinguish it from common writers. I meet with nothing to please me but the spiteful characters of the opposite party and its leaders. I expected much more secret history.

To THOMAS WHARTON

Dear Doctor

I am much concern'd to hear the account you give of yourself, & particularly for that dejection of spirits, which inclines you to see every thing in the worst light possible, and throw a sort of voluntary gloom not only over your present, but future days, as if even your situation now were not preferable to that of thousands round you, & as if your prospect hereafter might not open as much of happiness to you, as to any Person you know. The condition of our life perpetually instructs us to be rather slow to hope, as well as to despair, & (I know, you will forgive me, if I tell you) you are often a little too hasty in both, perhaps from constitution. It is sure, we have great power over our own minds, when we chuse to exert it; & tho it be difficult to resist the mechanic impulse & biass of our own temper, it is yet possible; & still more so, to delay those resolutions it inclines us to take, which always have cause to repent.

You tell me nothing of Mrs. Wharton's, or your own state of health. I will not talk to you more on this subject, till I hear you are both well, for that is the grand point, & without it we may as well not think at all. You flatter me in thinking, that any thing, I can do,[1] could at all alleviate the just concern your late loss has given you: but I can not flatter myself so far, & know how little qualified I am at present to give any satisfaction to myself on this head, & in this way, much less to you. I by no means pretend to inspiration, but yet I affirm, that the faculty in question is by no means voluntary. It is the result (I suppose) of a certain disposition of mind, which does not depend on oneself, & which I have not felt this long time. You that are a witness, how seldom this spirit has moved me in my life, may easily give credit to what I say.—

I am in hopes of seeing you very soon again in my way to Stoke.

---

1 Wharton had asked him to write an epitaph on his child.

Mrs. Rogers has been very ill this spring, & my other Aunt writes me word, that she herself has had something, (which she takes for a paralytic stroke) which came as she walk'd in the garden, & is afraid, she shall lose the use of one leg: so that it looks to me, as if I should have perhaps some years to pass in a house with two poor bed-ridden Women, a melancholy object, & one that in common humanity I can not avoid. I shall be glad to know, whether I can be in Gloucester-street for a week ten or twelve days hence.

I had wrote to you sooner, but that I have been on a little expedition lately to see Ely, Peterborough, Crowland-Abbey, Thorney, Fotheringhey, & many other old places, which has amused me a little.

Poor Mason is all alone at Aston (for his Curate is gone to be Tutor to somebody) with an inflammation in his eyes, & could scarce see to write a few lines. Adieu, Dear Sir, I am

Ever Yours

T G:

June 18. 1758.

To RICHARD STONHEWER

[*Stoke*] *August 18, 1758.*

I am as sorry as you seem to be, that our acquaintance harped so much on the subject of materialism, when I saw him with you in town, because it was plain to which side of the long-debated question he inclined. That we are indeed mechanical and dependent beings, I need no other proof than my own feelings; and from the same feelings I learn, with equal conviction, that we are not *merely* such: that there is a power within that struggles against the force and biass of that mechanism, commands its motion, and, by frequent practice, reduces it to that ready obedience which we call *Habit;* and all this in conformity to a preconceived opinion (no matter whether right or wrong) to that least material of all agents, a Thought. I have known many in his case who, while they thought they were conquering an old prejudice, did not perceive they were under the influence of one far more dangerous; one that furnishes us with a ready apology for all our worst actions, and opens to us a full licence for doing whatever we please; and yet these very people were not at all the more indulgent to other men (as they naturally should have been), their indignation to such as offended them, their desire of revenge on any body that hurt them was nothing mitigated: In short, the truth is, they wished to be persuaded of that opinion for the sake of its convenience, but were not so in their heart; and they would have been glad (as they ought in common prudence) that nobody else should think the same, for fear of the mischief that might ensue to themselves. His French Author I never saw, but have read fifty in the same strain, and shall read no more. I can be wretched enough without them. They put me in mind of the Greek Sophist that got immortal honour by discoursing so feelingly on the miseries of our condition, that fifty of his audience went home and hanged themselves; yet he lived himself (I suppose) many years after in very good plight.

You say you cannot conceive how Lord Shaftesbury came to be a Philosopher in vogue; I will tell you: First, he was a Lord; 2dly, he was as vain as any of his readers; 3dly, men are very prone to believe what they do not understand; 4thly, they will believe any thing at all, provided they are under no obligation to believe it; 5thly, they love to take a new road, even when that road leads no where; 6thly, he was reckoned a fine writer, and seemed always to mean more than he said. Would you have any more reasons? An interval of above forty years has pretty well destroyed the charm. A dead Lord ranks but with Commoners: Vanity is no longer interested in the matter, for the new road has become an old one. The mode of free-thinking is like that of Ruffs and Farthingales, and has given place to the mode of not thinking at all; once it was reckoned graceful, half to discover and half conceal the mind, but now we have been long accustomed to see it quite naked: primness and affection of style, like the good breeding of Queen Ann's Court, has turned to hoydening and rude familiarity.

To WILLIAM PALGRAVE

Stoke, Sept. 6, 1758.

I do not know how to make you amends, having neither rock, ruin, or precipice near me to send you; they do not grow in the south: but only say the word, if you would have a compact neat box of red brick with sash windows, or a grotto made of flints and shell-work, or a wallnut-tree with three mole-hills under it, stuck with honeysuckles round a bason of gold-fishes, and you shall be satisfied; they shall come by the Edinburgh coach.

In the meantime I congratulate you on your new acquaintance with the *savage*, the *rude,* and the *tremendous.* Pray, tell me, is it anything like what you had read in your book, or seen in two-shilling prints? Do not you think a man may be the wiser (I had almost said the better) for going a hundred or two of miles; and that the mind has more room in it than most people seem to think, if you will but furnish the apartments? I almost envy your last month, being in a very insipid situation myself; and desire you would not fail to send me some furniture for my Gothic apartment, which is very cold at present. It will be the easier task, as you have nothing to do but transcribe your little red books, if they are not rubbed out; for I conclude you have not trusted everything to memory, which is ten times worse than a lead pencil: Half a word fixed upon or near the spot, is worth a cart-load of recollection. When we trust to the picture that objects draw of themselves on our mind, we deceive ourselves; without accurate and particular observation, it is but ill-drawn at first, the outlines are soon blurred, the colours every day grow fainter; and at last, when we would produce it to any body, we are forced to supply its defects with a few strokes of our own imagination. God forgive me, I suppose I have done so myself before now, and misled many a good body that put their trust in me. Pray, tell me, (but with permission, and without any breach of hospitality), is it so much warmer on the other side of the Swale (as some people of honour say) than it is here? Has the singing of birds, the bleating of sheep, the lowing of herds, deafened you at Rainton? Did the vast old oaks and thick groves of Northumberland keep off the sun too much from you? I am too civil to extend my enquires beyond Berwick. Every thing, doubtless, must improve upon you as you advanced northward. You must tell me, though, about Melross, Rosslin Chapel, and Arbroath. In short, your Port-feuille must be so full, that I only desire a loose chapter or two, and will wait for the rest till it comes out.

To HORACE WALPOLE

[*c. April, 1760*].

I am so charmed with the two specimens of Erse poetry, that I cannot help giving you the trouble to enquire a little farther about them, and should wish to see a few lines of the original, that I may form some slight idea of the language, the measures, and the rhythm.

Is there anything known of the author or authors, and of what antiquity are they supposed to be?

Is there any more to be had of equal beauty, or at all approaching to it?

I have been often told that the poem called Hardicanute (which I always admired, and still admire) was the work of somebody that lived a few years ago. This I do not at all believe, though it has evidently been retouched in places by some modern hand: but, however, I am authorised by this report to ask, whether the two poems in question are certainly antique and genuine. I make this enquiry in quality of an antiquary, and am not otherwise concerned about it: for, if I were sure that any one now living in Scotland had written them to divert himself and laugh at the credulity of the world, I would undertake a journey into the Highlands only for the pleasure of seeing him.

To RICHARD STONHEWER

London, June 29, 1760.

Though you have had but a melancholy employment, it is worthy of envy, and (I hope) will have all the success it deserves. It was the best and most natural method of cure, and such as could not have been administered by any but your gentle hand. I thank you for communicating to me what must give you so much satisfaction.

I too was reading M. D'Alembert, and (like you) am totally disappointed in his Elements. I could only taste a little of the first course: it was dry as a stick, hard as a stone, and cold as a cucumber. But then the Letter to Rousseau is like himself; and the Discourses on Elocution, and on the Liberty of Music, are divine. He has added to his translations from Tacitus; and (what is remarkable) though that Author's manner more nearly resembles the best French Writers of the present age, than any thing, he totally fails in the attempt. Is it his fault, or that of the language?

I have received another Scotch packet with a third specimen, inferior in kind, (because it is merely description) but yet full of nature and noble wild imagination. Five Bards pass the night at the Castle of a Chief (himself a principal Bard); each goes out in his turn to observe the face of things, and returns with an extempore picture of the changes he has seen (it is an October night, the harvest-month of the Highlands). This is the whole plan; yet there is a contrivance, and a preparation of ideas, that you would not expect. The oddest thing is, that every one of them sees Ghosts (more or less). The idea, that struck and surprised me most, is the following. One of them (describing a storm of wind and rain) says

> Ghosts ride on the tempest to-night:
> Sweet is their voice between the gusts of wind;
> *Their songs are of other worlds!*

Did you never observe (*while rocking winds are piping loud*) that pause, as the gust is recollecting itself, and rising upon the ear in a shrill and plaintive note, like the swell of an Æolian harp? I do assure you there is nothing in the world so like the voice of a spirit. Thomson had an ear sometimes: he was not deaf to this; and has described it gloriously, but given it another different turn, and of more horrour. I cannot repeat the lines: it is in his Winter. There is another very fine picture in one of them. It describes the breaking of the clouds after the storm, before it is settled into a calm, and when the moon is seen by short intervals.

The waves are tumbling on the lake,
And lash the rocky sides.
The boat is brim-full in the cove,
The oars on the rocking tide.
Sad sits a maid beneath a cliff,
And eyes the rolling stream:
Her Lover promised to come,
She saw his boat (when it was evening) on the lake;
Are these his groans in the gale?
Is this his broken boat on the shore?

To JOHN CLERKE

Pembroke Hall, August 12, 1760.

Not knowing whether you are yet returned from your sea-water, I write at random to you. For me, I am come to my resting place, and find it very necessary, after living for a month in a house with three women that laughed from morning to night, and would allow nothing to the sulkiness of my disposition. Company and cards at home, parties by land and water abroad, and (what they call) *doing something,* that is, racketting about from morning to night, are occupations, I find, that wear out my spirits, especially in a situation where one might sit still, and be alone with pleasure; for the place was a hill like Clifden, opening to a very extensive and diversified landscape, with the Thames, which is navigable, running at its foot.

I would wish to continue here (in a very different scene, it must be confessed) till Michaelmas; but I fear I must come to town much sooner. Cambridge is a delight of a place, now there is nobody in it. I do believe you would like it, if you knew what it was without inhabitants. It is they, I assure you, that get it an ill name and spoil all. Our friend Dr. Chapman (one of its nuisances) is not expected here again in a hurry. He is gone to his grave with five mackerel (large and full of roe) in his belly. He eat them all at one dinner; but his fate was a turbot on Trinity Sunday, of which he left little for the company besides bones. He had not been hearty all the week; but after this sixth fish he never held up his head more, and a violent looseness carried him off.—They say he made a very good end.

Have you seen the Erse Fragments since they were printed? I am more puzzled than ever about their antiquity, though I still incline (against everybody's opinion) to believe them old. Those you have already seen are the best; though there are some others that are excellent too.

To WILLIAM MASON

[*c. August 31, 1760*].

A Note

Having made many enquiries about the authenticity of these Fragments; I have got a letter from Mr. David Hume (the Historian) which is more satisfactory than any thing I have yet met with on that subject. he says,

Certain it is, that these poems are in every bodys' mouth in the High-lands, have been handed down from Father to Son, & are of an age beyond all memory & tradition. Adam Smith, the celebrated Professor in Glasgow, told me, that the Piper of the Argyleshire Militia repeated to him all those, which Mr. Macpherson has translated, & many more of equal beauty. Major Mackay (Lord Rae's Brother) told me, that he remembers them perfectly well; as likewise did the Laird of Macfarline (the greatest Antiquarian we have in this country) & who insists strongly on the historical truth, as well as the poetical beauty of these productions. I could add the Laird & Lady Macleod, with many more, that live in different parts of the highlands, very remote from each other, & could only be acquainted with what had become (in a manner) national works. There is a Country-Surgeon in Lochaber, who has by heart the entire Epic Poem mention'd by Mr. Macpherson in his Preface, & as he is old; is perhaps the only person living, that knows it all; & has never committed it to writing; we are in the more hast to recover a Monument, which will certainly be regarded as a curiosity in the Republick of Letters: we have therefore set about a subscription of a Guinea or two Guineas apiece in order to enable Mr. Macpherson to undertake a Mission into the Highlands to recover this poem, & other fragments of antiquity.

I forgot to mention to you that the names of Fingal, Oscian, Oscur, &c: are still given in the Highlands to large Mastiffs, as we give to ours the names of Cæsar, Pompey, Hector &c.

To HORACE WALPOLE

[*December, 1760*].

I have been very ill this week with a great cold and a fever, and though now in a way to be well, am like to be confined some days longer: whatever you will send me that is new, or old, and *long,* will be received as a charity. Rousseau's people do not interest me; there is but one character and one style in them all, I do not know their faces asunder. I have no esteem for their persons or conduct, am not touched with their passions; and as to their story, I do not believe a word of it—not because it is improbable, but because it is absurd. If I had any little propensity, it was to Julie; but now she has gone and (so hand over head) married that monsieur de Wolmar, I take her for a *vraie Suissesse,* and do not doubt but she had taken a cup too much, like her lover. All this does not imply that I will not read it out, when you can spare the rest of it.

To THOMAS WHARTON

London. Jan. 31. 1761.

My dear Doctor

You seem to forget me: if it were for any other reason, than that you are very busy, that is, very happy, I should not so easily pass it over.

I send you a Swedish & English Calendar. the first Column is by Berger, a Disciple of Linnæus; the 2nd by Mr. Stillingfleet, the 3rd (very imperfect indeed) by me. You are to observe, as you tend your plantations & take your walks, how the Spring advances in the North, & whether Old-Park most resembles Upsal, or Stratton. This latter has on one side a barren black heath, on the other a light sandy loam; all the country about it is a dead flat. You see, it is necessary you should know the situation (I do not mean any reflection upon any body's place) & this is Mr. Stillingfleet's description of his Friend Mr. Marsham's Seat, to which in summer he retires, & botanizes. I have lately made an acquaintance with this Philosopher, who lives in a garret here in the winter, that he may support some near relations, who depend upon him. He is always employ'd, & always chearful, & seems to me a very worthy honest Man. His present scheme is to send some Persons properly qualified to reside a year or two in Attica to make themselves acquainted with the climate, productions, & natural history of the country, that we may understand Aristotle & Theophrastus, &c. who have been heathen-Greek to us for so many ages. This he has got proposed to Lord Bute, who is no unlikely Person to put it in execution, being himself a Botanist, & having now in the press a new System of Botany of his own writing in several volumes, the profits of which he gives to Dr. Hill (the Inspector) who has lately got the place of Master-Gardiner at Kensington, reckon'd worth near 2000£ a-year. There is an odd thing for you!

One hears nothing of the K., but what gives one the best opinion of him imaginable: I hope, it may hold. The R. F. run loose about the world, & people do not know how to treat them, nor they how to be treated. They visit & are visited: some come to the Street-door to receive them, & that, they say, is too much: others to the head of the stairs, & that they think too little. no body sits down with them, not even in their own house, unless at a card-table, so the world are like to grow very weary of the honour. none but the D. of Y. enjoy themselves (you know, he always did) but the world seems weary of this honour too, for a different reason. I have just heard no bad story of him. When he was at Southampton in the summer, there was a Clergy-man in the neighbourhood with two very handsome daughters. He had soon wind of them, & drop'd in for some reason or other, came again & again, & grew familiar enough to eat a bone of their mutton. At last he said to the Father, Miss—— lead a mighty confined life here always at home, why can't you let one of them go, & take an airing now and then with me in my chaise? Ah! Sir (says the Parson) do but look at them, a couple of hale fresh-colour'd hearty Wenches! They need no airing, they are well-enough: but there is their Mother, poor Woman, has been in a declining way many years. If your R. H. would give her an airing now & then, it would be doing us a great kindness indeed!

You see, old Wortley-Montagu is dead at last at 83. It was not mere avarice, & its companion, abstinence, that kept him alive so long. He every day drank (I think, it was) half a pint of Tokay, which he imported himself from Hungary in greater quantity than he could use, & sold the Overplus for any price he chose to set upon it. He has left better than half a million of money: to Lady Mary 1200£ a-year, in case she gives up her pretensions to dowry; & if not, it comes to his Son. To the same Son 1000£ per an. for life only, & after him to his Daughter, Lady Bute. (Now this Son is about 80,000£ in debt) to all Lady Bute's Children, which are eleven, 2000£ a-piece. *All the remainder* to Lady Bute, & after her to her second Son, who takes the name of Wortley, & (if he fail) to the next in order; & after all these & their Children to Lord Sandwich, to whom *in present* he leaves some old Manuscripts. Now I must tell you a story of Lady Mary. As she was on her travels, she had occasion to go somewhere by sea, & (to save charges) got a passage on board a Man of War: the ship was (I think) Commodore Barnet's. When he had landed her, she told him, she knew she was not to offer to pay for her passage, but in consideration of his many civilities entreated him to wear a ring for her sake, & press'd him to accept it, which he did. It was an emerald of remarkable size & beauty. Some time after, as he wore it, some Friend was admiring it, & asking how he came by it. When he heard from whom it came, he laugh'd & desired him to shew it to a Jeweller, whom he knew. The Man was sent for: he unset it; it was a paste not worth 40 shillings.

The Ministry are much out of joint. Mr. P.[1] much out of humour, his popularity tottering, chiefly occasion'd by a Pamphlet against the German War, written by that *squeaking* acquaintance of ours, Mr. Mauduit: it has had a vast run. The Irish are very intractable, even the Lords Justices themselves; great difficulties about who shall be sent over to tame them: my Lord Holdernesse again named, but (I am told) has refused it. Every body waits for a new Parliament to settle their ideas.

I have had no gout, since you went: I will not brag, lest it return with redoubled violence. I am very foolish, & do nothing to mark, that I ever was: I am going to Cambridge to take the *fresh air* this fine winter for a month or so. We have had snow one day this winter, but it did not lie: it was several months ago. The 18th of Jan. I took a walk to *Kentish-Town,* wind N.W., bright & frosty. Therm. at Noon was at 42. The grass remarkably green & flourishing. I observed, on dry banks facing the South that Chickweed, Dandelion, Groundsel, Red Archangel, & Shepherds-Purse were beginning to flower. This is all I know of the Country.

My best compliments to Mrs. Wharton. I hear her butter is the best in the Bishoprick, & that even Deborah has learn'd to spin. I rejoice you are all in health, but why are you deaf: & blind too, or you could not vote for F. V.! I have abundance more to say, but my paper won't hear of it. Adieu!

---

[1] Pitt.

To THOMAS WHARTON

Dear Doctor

When I received your letter I was still detain'd in Town: but am now at last got to Cambridge. I applied immediately to Dr. Ashton (who was nearest at hand) for information as to the expences of Eton without naming any one's name. He returned me the *civilest* of answers, & that if the boy was to be on the foundation, I had no more to do but send him to him, & the business should be done. As to the charges, he was going to Eton, & would send me an account from thence; which he did accordingly on Sunday last, & here it is inclosed with his second letter. You will easily conceive, that there must be additional expences, that can be reduced to no rules, as pocketmoney, cloths, books, &c. & which are left to a Father's own discretion.

My notion is, that your Nephew being an only Son, & rather of a delicate constitution, ought not to be exposed to the hardships of the College. I know, that the expence in that way is much lessen'd; but your Brother has but one Son, & can afford to breed him an Oppidant.[1] I know, that a Colleger is sooner form'd to scuffle in the world, that is, by drubbing & tyranny is made more hardy or more cunning, but these in my eyes are no such desirable acquisitions: I know too, that a certain (or very probable) provision for life is a thing to be wish'd: but you must remember, what a thing a fellow of King's is. In short you will judge for yourselves. If you accept my *good Friend's* offer, I will proceed accordingly: if not, we will thank him, & willingly let him recommend to us a cheap boarding-house, not disdaining his protection & encouragement, if it can be of any little use to your Nephew. He has married one of Amyand's Sisters with 12,000£. (I suppose, you know her; she is an enhancing object!), & he is settled in the Preachership of Lincolns Inn.

Sure Mr. Jon. or some one has told you, how your *good Friend,* Mr. L. has been horsewhip'd, trampled, bruised, & piss'd

---

[1] A student not on the foundation, who boards in the town.

upon, by a Mrs. Mackenzie, a sturdy Scotch Woman. It was done in an Inn-yard at Hampstead in the face of day, & he has put her in the Crown-Office. It is very true. I will not delay this letter to tell you any more stories. Adieu! I am ever

Yours

T G.

Pembroke-Hall.

June 23. 1761.

Mr. Brown, (the *petit bon-homme*) joins his compliments to mine, & presents them to you and Mrs. Wharton.

I have been dreadfully disappointed in Rousseau's Heloïse: but Mason admires it.

To THOMAS WHARTON

[*September 8, 1761*].

Dear Doctor

I am just come to Town, where I shall stay six weeks or more, & (if you will send your dimensions) will look out for papers[1] at the shops. I own I never yet saw any Gothic papers to my fancy. There is one fault, that is in the nature of the thing, & can not be avoided. The great beauty of all Gothick designs is the variety of perspectives they occasion. This a Painter may represent on the walls of a room in some measure; but not a Designer of Papers, where, what is represented on one breadth, must be exactly repeated on another, both in the light & shade, and in the dimensions. This we can not help; but they do not even do what they might: they neglect Hollar, to copy Mr. Halfpenny's architecture, so that all they do is more like a goosepie than a cathedral. You seem to suppose, that they do Gothic papers in colours, but I never saw any but such as were to look like Stucco: nor indeed do I conceive that they could have any effect or meaning. Lastly, I never saw any thing of gilding, such as you mention, on paper, but we shall see. Only pray leave as little to my judgement as possible.

---

[1] Wallpapers.

I thank'd Dr. Ashton before you told me to do so. He writes me word, that (except the first Sunday of a month) he believes, he shall be at Eton till the middle of November; & (as he now knows the person in question is your nephew) adds, I remember Dr. Wharton with great pleasure, & beg you will signify as much to him, when you write.

The King is just married, it is the hottest night in the year. Adieu, it is late, I am ever

yours
T G:

To JAMES BROWN

Sept. 24. 1761. London.

Dear Sir

I set out at half an hour past four in the morning for the Coronation, & (in the midst of perils & dangers) arrived very safe at my Lord Chamberlain's Box in Westminster Hall. it was on the left hand of the throne over that appropriated to the Foreign Ministers. Opposite to us was the Box of the Earl Marshal, & other Great Officers, & below it that of the Princess, & younger Part of the Royal Family. Next them was the royal sideboard. Then below the steps of the Haut-pas were the tables of the Nobility on each side quite to the door, behind them boxes for the sideboards, over these the galleries for the Peers Tickets, & still higher the boxes of the Auditor, the board of Green-Cloth, &c. all these throng'd with people head above head, all dress'd, & the Women with their Jewels on. In the front of the throne was a Triomfe of foliage & flowers, resembling nature, placed on the royal table, & rising as high as the canopy itself. The several bodies, that were to form the procession, issued from behind the throne gradually & in order, and proceeding down the steps were ranged on either side of the hall, all the Privy-Councellors, that are Commoners, (I think) were there, (except Mr. Pitt), mightily dress'd in rich stuffs of gold & colour with long flowing wigs, some of them comical figures enough. the Knights of the Bath with their high plumage were very ornamental, of the Scotch Peers or Peeresses, that you see in the list, very few walk'd; & of the English Dowagers as few, tho' many of them were in Town & among the Spectators. The noblest and most graceful figures among the Ladies, were the Marchioness of Kildare (as Viscountess Leinster) Viscountess Spencer, Countesses of Harrington, Pembroke & Strafford, & the Duchess of Richmond. of the older sort (for there is a grace, that belongs to age too) the Countess of Westmoreland Countess of Abermarle, & Duchess of Queensberry. I should mention too the odd and extraordinary appearances: they were the Viscountess Say & Sele, Countesses of Portsmouth, & another that I do not name, because she is said to be an extraordinary good woman, Countess of Harcourt, & Dutchess of St. Albans. Of the Men doubtless the noblest and most striking figure was the Earl of Errol, & after him the Dukes of Ancaster, Richmond, Marlborough, Kingston; Earl of Northampton, Pomfret, Viscount Weymouth, &c. The comical Men were the Earl Talbot (most in sight of anybody) Earls of Delawere & Macclesfield, Lords Montfort & Melcombe. All these I beheld at great leisure. Then the Princess and Royal Family enter'd their Box; the Queen, & then the King, took their places in their chairs of state, glitt'ring with jewels (for the hire of which, besides all his own, he paid 9000£) & the Dean & Chapter (who had been waiting without doors a full hour & half) brought up the Regalia, which the D. of Ancaster received and placed on the Table. Here ensued great confusion in the delivering them out to the Lords, who were appointed to bear them. The Heralds were stupid; the Great Officers knew nothing they were doing; the Bishop of Rochester would have drop'd the Crown, if it had not been pin'd to the Cushion, & the King was often obliged to call out, & set matters right: but the Sword of State had been entirely forgot; so Lord Huntingdon was forced to carry the Lord Mayor's great two-handed sword instead of it. This made it later than ordinary, before they got under their canopies, & set forward. I should have told you, that the old Bishop of Lincoln with his stick went doddling by the side of the Queen, & the Bishop of Chester had the pleasure of bearing the gold paten. When they were gone we went down to dinner, for there were three rooms below, where the Duke of Devonshire was so good to feed us with great cold Sirloins of beef, legs of mutton, fillets of veal, & other substantial viands, and liqueurs, which we devour'd all higgledy-piggledy like Porters. After which every one scrambled up again & seated themselves. The tables were now spread, the cold viands set on & at the Kings table & side-board a great show of gold-plate, & a desert representing Parnassus with abundance of figures of Muses, Arts, &c. design'd by Lord Talbot: this was so high, that those at the end of the Hall could see neither K. nor Queen at supper. When they return'd it was dark, that the People without doors scarce saw anything of the procession, & as the Hall had then no other light than two long ranges of candles at each of the Peers tables, we saw almost as little as they; only one perceived the Lords & Ladies sidleing in & taking their places to dine, but the instant the Queen's Canopy enter'd, fire was given to all the Lustres at once by trains of prepared flax, that reached from one to the other. To me it seem'd an interval of not half a minute, before the whole was in a blaze of splendor. It is true, that for that half minute it rain'd fire upon the heads of all the spectators (the flax falling in large flakes) & the Ladies (Queen & all) were in no small terrors, but no mischief ensued. It was out as soon as it fell, & the most magnificent spectacle, I ever beheld remain'd. The K. (bowing to the Lords as he pass'd) with his crown on his head, & the sceptre & orb in his hands, took his place with great majesty & grace: so did the Q. with her crown, sceptre & rod. Then supper was served in gold plate, the Earl Talbot, D. of Bedford, & E. of Effingham, in their robes, all three on horseback prancing & curvetting, like the hobby-horses in the Rehearsal, usher'd in the courses to the foot of the haut-pas. Between the courses the Champion performed his part with applause. the E. of Denbigh carved for the King, E. of Holdernesse for the Queen: they both eat like farmers. At the board's end on the right sup'd the D.'s of York & Cumberland, on the left Lady Augusta, all of them very rich in jewels. The maple cups, the wafers, the faulcons, &c. were brought up & presented in form, 3 persons were knighted, & before 10 the K. & Q. retired. Then I got a scrap of supper, & at one o'clock I walk'd home. So much for the spectacle, which in magnificence surpass'd every thing I have seen. Next I must tell you, that the Barons of the Cinque-ports, who by ancient right should dine at a table on the Haut-pas at the right hand of the throne, found that no provision at all had been made for them, & representing their case to Earl Talbot, he told them Gentlemen, if you speak to me as High-Steward I must tell you, there was no room for you: if as Lord Talbot, I am ready to give you satisfaction in any way you think fit. They are several of them Gentlemen of the best families, so this has bred ill blood. In the next place the City of London found they had no table neither; but Beckford bullied my Lord High Steward, till he was forced to give them that intended for the Knights of the Bath & instead of it they dined at the entertainment prepared for the Great Officers. 3dly & lastly (this is fact) when the Queen retired while she was in the Abbey, to a sort of closet furnish'd with necessary conveniences, one of the Ladies opening the door to see all was right, found the D. of Newcastle perk'd up & in the very act upon the anointed velvet closestool. Do not think I joke, it is literally true.

Bussy was not at the ceremony: he is just setting out for France. Spain has supplied them with money, & is picking a quarrel with us about the fishery & the logwood. Mr Pitt says, so much the better! & was for recalling Lord Bristol directly: however a flat denial has been return'd to their pretentions.

When you have read this send it to Pa.

To THOMAS WHARTON

Oct. 22, 1761. Southern Row.

Dear Doctor

Do not think me very dilatory, for I have been sending away all my things from this house (where nevertheless I shall continue while I stay in Town) & have besides been confined with a severe cold to my room. On rummageing Mr Bromwich's & several other shops I am forced to tell you, that there are absolutely no papers at all, that deserve the name of Gothick, or that you would bear the sight of. They are all what they call *fancy,* & indeed resemble nothing that ever was in use in any age or country. I am going to advise, what perhaps you may be deter'd from by the addition of expence, but what, in your case I should certainly do. Any body that can draw the least in the world is capable of sketching in Indian ink a compartment or two of diaper-work, or a nich or tabernacle with its fretwork: take such a Man with you to Durham-Cathedral, & let him copy one division of any ornament you think will have any effect, from the high-altar suppose or the nine altars, or what you please. If nothing there suits you, chuse in Dart's Canterbury or Dugdale's Warwickshire, &c. & send the design hither. They will execute it here, & make a new stamp on purpose, provided you will take 20 pieces of it, & it will come to ½ or a penny a yard the more (according to the work, that is in it). This I really think worth your while. I mention your doing it there, because it will be then under your own eye, & at your own choice, & you can proportion the whole better to the dimensions of your room, for if the design be of arcade work, or any thing on a pretty large scale, & the arches or niches are to rise one above the other, there must be some contrivance, that they may fill the entire space & not be cut in sunder and incompleat . . . this indeed, where the work is in small compartments, is not to be minded. Say therefore, if you come into this; or shall I take a Man here to Westminster, & let him copy some of those fret-works? Tho' I think, in the books I have named you may find better things. I much doubt of the effect colours (any other than the tints of stucco) would have in a gothic design on paper, & here they have nothing to judge from. Those I spoke of at Ely were green & pale blue with the raised work white, if you care to hazard it. I saw an all-silver paper quite plain, & it look'd like block-tin. In short there is nothing I would venture to send you.

One of 3d a yard in small compartments thus, might perhaps do for the stairs, but very likely it is common, & besides it is not pure gothick, therefore I would not send it alone.
Adieu & tell me soon what I shall do.
I go to Camb. in 3 weeks or less.

To THOMAS WHARTON

Nov. 13, 1761. London.

Dear Doctor

I went as soon as I received your last letter, to chuse papers for you at Bromwich's. I applaud your determination, for it is mere pedantry in Gothicism to stick to nothing but altars & tombs, & there is no end of it, if we are to sit upon nothing but Coronation-chairs., nor drink out of nothing but chalices & flagons. The idea is sufficiently kept up, if we live in an ancient house, but with modern conveniences about us. Nobody will expect the inhabitants to wear ruffs & farthingales. Besides these things are not to be had, unless we make them ourselves.

I have however ventured to bespeak (for the staircase) the stucco-paper of 3d a yard, which I mention'd to you before. It is rather pretty, & nearly Gothick. The border is entirely so, & where it runs horizontally, will be very proper; where perpendicularly, not altogether so: I do not see, how this could be avoided. The crimson paper is the handsomest I ever saw; from its simplicity, I believe, as it is nothing but the same thing repeated throughout. Mr. Trevor (Hambden) design'd it for his own use. The border is a spiral scroll, also the prettiest I have seen. This paper is 8d. a yard. The blew is the most extravagant, a mohair-flock paper of a shilling a yard, which I fear you will blame me for; but it was so handsome, & look'd so warm, I could not resist it. The pattern is small, & will look like a cut-velvet: the border a scroll like the last, but on a larger scale. You will ask, why the crimson (which was to be the best) is not a mohair-paper too? Because it would have no effect in that sort of pattern; & it is as handsome as it need to be, without that expence. The library paper is a cloth-colour: all I can say for it is, that it was the next best design they had after the former. I think it is 7d½ a yard. They do not keep any quantity by them (only samples of each sort) but promise, they shall be finish'd in a week, & sent to your Brother's, with whom I have left the bill, as I go myself to Cambridge in a day or two. Indeed this is a very improper time to trouble him, tho' when I call'd there last night, I was told she was a great *deal better.* I did not know of his loss till you told me: on which I went to ask how they did, & found him truly in a very deplorable situation. He said he had wrote to you, but I do not know, whether he was able to give you a full acco—

To THOMAS WHARTON

[*Cambridge, December 4, 1762*].

Dear Doctor

I feel very ungrateful every day, that I continue silent, & yet I do not write to you: but now the pen is in my hand, and I am in for it. When I left you, in spite of the rain I went out of my way to Richmond, & made a shift to see the Castle, & look down upon the valley, thro' which the Swale winds: that was all the weather would permitt. At Rippon I visited the Church, which we had neglected before, with some pleasure, & saw the Ure full to its brink & very inclinable to overflow. Some faint gleams of sunshine gave me an opportunity of walking over Studley, & descending into the ruins of Fountain's Abbey, which I examined with attention. I pass'd over the ugly moor of Harrowgate, made a bow to the Queen's-Head, & got late at night to Leedes: here the rain was so perverse I could scarce see the Town, much less go to Kirkstall-Abbey, which was my intention; so I proceeded to Wakefield, & Wentworth Castle. Here the Sun again indulged me, & open'd as beautiful a scene of rich & cultivated country, as (I am told) Yorkshire affords. The water is all artificial, but with an air of nature; much wood; a very good house in the Q. Anne style, which is now new-fronting in a far better taste by the present Earl; many pictures not worth a farthing,

& a castle built only for a play-thing on the top of the hill as a point of view, & to command a noble prospect. I went on to Sheffield, liked the situation in a valley by a pretty river's side, surrounded with charming hills: saw the handsome parish-church with the chappel & monuments of the Talbots. Then I enter'd the Peak, a countrey beyond comparison uglier than any other I have seen in England, black, tedious, barren, and not mountainous enough to please one with its horrors. This is mitigated, since you were there, by a road like a bowling green, which soon brought me to Chatsworth. The house has the air of a Palace, the hills rising on three of its sides shut out the view of its dreary neighbourhood, & are cover'd with wood to their tops: the front opens to the Derwent winding thro' the valley, which by the art of Mr. Brown is now always visible & full to its brim. For heretofore it could not well be seen (but in rainy seasons) from the windows. A handsome bridge is lately thrown over it, & the stables taken away, which stood full in view between the house & the river. The prospect opens here to a wider tract of country terminated by more distant hills: this scene is yet in its infancy, the objects are thinly scatter'd, & the clumps and plantations lately made: but it promises well in time. Within doors the furniture corresponds to the stateliness of the appartments, fine tapestry, marble doorcases with fruit, flowers, & foliage, excellently done by Old Cibber's Father, windows of plate-glass in gilded frames, & such a profusion of Gibbons' best carving in wood, viz. Dead-Game, fish, shells, flowers, &c. as I never saw anywhere. The cielings & staircases all painted by Verrio or Laguerre, in their usual sprawling way, & no other pictures, but in one room 8 or 10 portraits, some of them very good, of James & Charles, the first's time. The gardens are small, & in the French style with water-works, particularly a grand Cascade of steps & a *Temple d'eaux* at the head of it. From thence I went to Hardwick. One would think Mary, Queen of Scots, was but just walk'd down into the Park with her Guard for half-an-hour. Her Gallery, her room of audience, her antichamber, with the very canopies, chair of state, footstool, Lit-de-repos, Oratory, carpets, & hangings, just as she left them. A little tatter'd indeed, but the more venerable; & all preserved with religious care, & paper'd up in winter. The park & country are just like Hertfordshire. I went by Chesterfield & Mansfield to revisit my old friend the Trent at Nottingham, where I passed 2 or 3 days, & from thence took stage-coach to London.

When I arrived there, I found Professor Turner had been dead above a fortnight, & being cocker'd and spirited up by some Friends (tho' it was rather of the latest) I got my name suggested to Lord B. You may easily imagine, who undertook it; & indeed he did it with zeal. I received my answer very soon, which was what you may easily imagine, but join'd with great professions of *his desire to serve me* on any future occasion, & many more fine words, that I pass over, not out of modesty, but for another reason. So you see I have made my fortune, like Sir Fr. Wronghead. This *nothing* is a profound secret, and no one here suspects it even now: today I hear, that Delaval has got it, but we are not yet certain: next to myself I wish'd for him.

You see we have made a peace. I shall be silent about it, because if I say anything antiministerial, you will tell me, you know the reason; & if I approve it, you will tell me, I have expectations still. All I know is, that the D. of Newcastle & Lord Hardwick both say, it is an excellent Peace; & only Mr. Pitt calls it inglorious & insidious.

I had a little Gout twice, while I was in Town, which confined me some time: yet I bespoke your chairs. They are what is call'd *Rout-Chairs,* but as they are to be a little better in shape & materials than ordinary, will come to about 6s 9d a chair. I desired your Brother to judge, how he perform'd, & the first, that was made, was to be sent him to see.

My best respects attend Mrs. Wharton, who I suppose, receives them in bed. How does she doe? My compliments to Miss. I am ever truly

Yours

Mason is in Yorkshire now, but I miss'd of him.

To THOMAS WHARTON

[*Pembroke, August 5, 1763*].

Dear Doctor

You may well wonder at my long taciturnity: I wonder too, & know not what cause to assign, for it is certain, I think of you daily. I believe, it is owing to the nothingness of my history, for except six weeks that I pass'd in Town towards the end of spring, & a little jaunt to Epsom & Box-Hill, I have been here time out of mind in a place, where no events grow, tho' we preserve those of former days by way of *Hortus Siccus* in our libraries. My slumbers were disturbed the other day by an unexpected visit from Mr. W. who dined with me, seem'd mighty happy for the time he stay'd, & said he could like to live here: but hurried home in the evening to his new Gallery, which is all Gothicism, & gold, & crimson, & looking-glass. He has purchased at an auction in Suffolk ebony-chairs & old moveables enough to load a waggon.

Mason & I have received letters from Count Algarotti, Chambellan de sa Majeste le Roi de Prusse, with observations, (that is panegyricks) on our Tragedies & our Odes, & a present of certain Italian Dissertations, which he has lately publish'd on the state of Painting and Musick. One of them is dedicated to Mr. Pitt, whom he styles—*Uomo immortale, e Restitutore d'Inghilterra, Amico del gran Federigo.*

I was in Town, when Mr. Middleton died, & immediately got all the information I could (first from Stonhewer & then from your Brother) of the disposition he had made. I suppose, they are as good as you expected, & tho' the prospect is but small, that you should enjoy the benefit of them in your own person, yet that is not impossible; & your Son (I think) stands a very good chance, which can not chuse but open an agreeable prospect to you, in which I take a part, & congratulate you both upon it. I doubt you have not read Rousseau's *Emile*: every body that has children, should read it more than once, for tho' it abounds with his usual glorious absurdity, tho' his general scheme of education be an impracticable chimera: yet there are a thousand lights struck out, a thousand important truths better express'd than ever they were before, that may be of service to the wisest Man. Particularly I think he has observed children with more attention & knows their meaning & the working of their little passions better than any other Writer. As to his religious discussions, which have alarmed the world, & engaged their thoughts more than any other part of his book, I set them all at nought, & wish they had been omitted. Mrs. Jonathan told me, you begun your evening-prayer as soon as I was gone, & that it had a great effect upon the congregation: I hope you have not grown weary of it, nor lay it aside, when company comes. Poor Mrs. Bonfoy (who taught me to pray) is dead. She struggled near a week against the Iliac Passion (I fear) in great torture with all her senses about her, & with much resolution took leave of her physician some days before she expired, & would suffer no one to see her afterwards but common Servants.

You describe Winston *con tanto amore,* that I take it amiss I was not suffer'd to see it, & want to be buried there too. But enough of death! I have forgot to tell you that Dr. Long has had an audience of the K. & Queen an hour long at Bucking-ham-House. His errand was to present them with a Lyricord (such a one!) of his own making, & a glass-sphere: he had long been solliciting this honour, which Lord Bute at last procured him, & he is very happy. The K. told him, he bid fair for a century of life at least; ask'd him, whether he preach'd; why he did not write verses in the Cambridge Collection; & what not? The Q. spoke French to him, & ask'd, how he liked Handel?

And I ask you, how you like the present times? Whether you had not rather be a Printer's Devil, than a Secretary of State? You are to expect (I hear) a new Ministry, composed of the Earl of Shelburne, Mr. Rigby, Duke & Dutchess of Bedford, Earl Gower, &c. which doubtless will give universal satisfaction. The great Lord Holland, who is at Paris, being lately asked by a young Man, who was returning home, whether he had any commands in England, made no reply but by shrugging up his shoulders, & fetching a deep sigh.

I kept an exact account of Heat & Cold in the Spring here: the sum & substance of which is, that (at 9 in the morning) on the 18th of January, the Therm. was at 31, & the small birds were so tame you might take them up with your hand. This was the greatest cold. On the 15th of April it was at 58, & the same afternoon at 65, which was the greatest heat from Jan. 1 to May 1st.

Feb. 3. Snowdrops flower'd.
12. Crocus & Hepatica fl., the snow then lieing, & Therm. at 45.
18. Chaffinch sings. Bees appear.
21. White butterfly abroad.
25. Gnats flie, & large Flies. Mezereon fl.
27. Honeysuckle & Gooseberry unfold their leaves.

March 1. Violet flowers (in the garden). Rose opens its leaf.
3. Daffodil & single Hyacinth fl. Spider spins.
5. Thrush singing.
6. Elder in leaf, Currant & Weeping Willow in l.
8. Apricot blows. Sky-Lark singing.
11. Wind very high at S.E., which continued with hard frost.
16. Frost gone.
18. Abricot in full bloom.
19. Almond flowers. Lilac, Barberry & Gelder-rose in leaf.

April 2. Standard-Abricot, & Wall-Pears flower. Quince, Apple, and Sweet-briar, in leaf. Currant flowers. Dutch-Elm opens its leaf.
4. Plumb in leaf.
5. Crown Imperial fl.
6. Plumb flowers. Hawthorn, Horse-Chestnut, Mountain-Ash, in leaf.
9. Lime-tree in leaf. Jonquil & single Anemone flower. Lady-birds seen.

11. Cowslip flowers, & Auricula. Swallow appears. young Rooks caw in the nest.
14. Red-Start appears. Cherries in full bloom.
15. Frontignac Vine in leaf. Double Wall-flower blows.
16. Nightingale sings. Apple blossoms.
17. Chaffinch & Red-Start sit on their eggs.
20. Elm, Willow, & Ash, in flower (with the Black-thorn) Hawthorn in full leaf.
21. Sycomore quite green. Oak puts out.

Pray present my respects to Mrs. & Miss Wharton. I am ever
Sincerely Yours.

We have nothing but rain & thunder of late.

To COUNT ALGAROTTI

Cambridge, Sept. 9, 1763.

Sir

I received some time since the unexpected honour of a Letter from you, & the promise of a pleasure, which till of late I had not the opportunity of enjoying. Forgive me if I make my acknowledgements in my native tongue, as I see it is perfectly familiar to you, & I (tho not unacquainted with the writings of Italy) should from disuse speak its Language with an ill grace, & with still more constraint to one, who possesses it in all its strength & purity.

I see with great satisfaction your efforts to reunite the congenial arts of Poetry, Musick, & the Dance, which with the assistance of Painting & Architecture, regulated by Taste, & supported by magnificence & power, might form the noblest scene, and bestow the sublimest pleasure, that the imagination can conceive. but who shall realize these delightful visions? There is, I own, one Prince in Europe, that wants neither the will, the spirit, nor the ability: but can he call up Milton from his grave, can he reanimate Marcello, or bid the Barberina or the Sallé move again? Can he (as much a King as he is) govern an Italian

Virtuosa, destroy her caprice & impertinence without hurting her talents, or command those unmeaning graces & tricks of voice to be silent, that have gain'd her the adoration of her own country?

One cause that so long has hindered, & (I fear) will hinder that happy union, which you propose, seems to me to be this: that Poetry (which, as you allow, must lead the way, & direct the operations of the subordinate Arts) implies at least a liberal education, a degree of literature, & various knowledge, whereas the others (with a few exceptions) are in the hands of Slaves & Mercenaries, I mean, of People without education, who, tho neither destitute of Genius, nor insensible to fame, must yet make gain their principal end, & subject themselves to the prevailing taste of those, whose fortune only distinguishes them from the Multitude.

I cannot help telling you, that 8 or 10 years ago, I was a witness of the power of your comic musick. There was a little troop of Buffi, that exhibited a Burletta in London, not in the Opera-House, where the audience is chiefly of the better sort, but in one of the common theatres full of all kinds of people & (I believe) the fuller from that natural aversion we bear to Foreigners: their looks & their noise made it evident, they did not come thither to hear; & on similar occasions I have known candles lighted, broken bottles, & penknives flung on the stage, the benches torn up, the scenes hurried into the street & set on fire. The curtain drew up, the musick was of Cocchi with a few airs of Pergolesi interspersed. The Singers were (as usual) deplorable, but there was one Girl (she call'd herself the Niccolina) with little voice & less beauty; but with the utmost justness of ear, the strongest expression of countenance, the most speaking eyes, the greatest vivacity & variety of gesture. Her first appearance instantly fix'd their attenion; the tumult sunk at once, or if any murmur rose, it was soon hush'd by a general cry for silence. Her first air ravish'd every body; they forgot their prejudices, they forgot, that they did not understand a word of the language; they enter'd into all the humour of the part, made her repeat all her songs, & continued their transports, their laughter, & applause to the end of the piece. Within these three last years the Paganina & Amici have met with almost the same applause once a week from a politer audience on the Opera-stage. The truth is, the Opera itself, tho supported here at a great expence for so many years, has rather maintain'd itself by the admiration bestow'd on a few particular voices, or the borrow'd taste of a few Men of condition, that have learn'd in Italy how to admire, than by any genuine love we bear to the best Italian musick: nor have we yet got any style of our own, & this I attribute in great measure to the language, which in spite of its energy, plenty, & the crowd of excellent Writers this nation has produced, does yet (I am sorry to say it) retain too much of its barbarous original to adapt itself to musical composition. I by no means wish to have been born any thing but an Englishman; yet I should rejoice to exchange tongues with Italy.

Why this Nation has made no advances hitherto in painting & sculpture is hard to say. The fact is undeniable, & we have the vanity to apologize for ourselves, as Virgil did for the Romans, *Excudent alii,* &c. It is sure that Architecture had introduced itself in the reign of the unfortunate Charles the first, & Inigo Jones has left us some few monuments of his skill, that shew him capable of greater things. Charles had not only a love for the beautiful arts, but some taste in them. The confusion, that soon follow'd, swept away his magnificent collection, the artists were dispersed or ruin'd, & the arts disregarded till very lately. The young Monarch now on the throne is said to esteem & understand them: I wish he may have the leisure to cultivate, & the skill to encourage them with due regard to merit, otherwise it is better to neglect them. You, Sir, have pointed out the true Sources & the best examples to your Countrymen. They have nothing to do, but to be what they once were; and yet perhaps it is more difficult to restore Good taste to a nation, that has degenerated, than to indroduce it in one, where as yet it has never flourish'd. You are generous enough to wish, & sanguine to forsee, that it shall one day flourish in England. I too must wish, but can hardly extend my hopes so far. It is well for us that you do not see our publick exhibitions—but our Artists are yet in their infancy, & therefore I will not absolutely despair.

I owe to Mr. Howe the honour I have of conversing with Count Algarotti, & it seems as if I meant to indulge myself in the opportunity: but I have done, Sir. I will only add, that I am proud of your approbation having no relish for any other fame than what is confer'd by the few real Judges, that are so thinly scatter'd over the face of the earth. I am, Sir, with great respect

Your most obliged humble servant

T GRAY

To WILLIAM MASON

Saturday, Oct. [*8, 1763*] *Pemb. Coll.*

Dear Mason

I rejoice. But has she common sense, is she a Gentlewoman? Has she money? Has she a nose? I know, she sings a little, & twiddles on the harpsichord, hammers at sentiment, & puts herself in an attitude, admires a cast in the eye, & can say Elfrida by heart: but these are only the virtues of a Maid. Do let her have some wifelike qualities, & a double portion of prudence, as she will have not only herself to govern, but you also, & that with an absolute sway. Your Friends, I doubt not, will suffer for it: however we are very happy, & have no other wish than to see you settled in the world. We beg you would not stand fiddleing about it, but be married forthwith, & then take chaise, and come consummating all the way to Cambridge to be touch'd by Mr. Brown, & so to London, where to be sure she must pass the first winter. If good reasons (& not your own, nor her Coquetry) forbid this: yet come hither yourself, for our Copuses and Welch Rabbets are impatient for you.

I have compared Helvetius & Elfrida, and find thirteen parallel passages, five of which at least are so direct & close, as to leave no shadow of a doubt, & therefore confirm all the rest. it is a Phænomenon, that you will be in the right to inform yourself about, & that I long to understand. Another Phænomenon is, that I read it without finding it out. All I remember is, that I thought it not at all *English,* & did not much like it; and the reason is plain; for the lyric flights & choral flowers suited not at all with the circumstances or character, as he had contrived it.

I sent your letter to Algarotti directly. My *Coserelle* came a long while ago; from Mr. Holles, I suppose; who sent me (without a name), a set of his engravings, when I was last in Town, which (I reckon) is what you mean by your fine presents. The *Congresso di Citera* was not one of the books: that was my mistake. I like his treatises very well.

I hope in God the dedicatorial Sonnet has not staid for me. I object nothing to the 2d line, but like it the better for Milton, and with him I would read in penult: (give me a shilling) *his ghastly smile,* &c.: but if you won't put it in, then read *wonted* smile, & a little before *secure from envy.* I see nothing to alter. What I said was the best line is the best line still. do come hither, & I will read and criticize

Your amorous ditties all a winter's day.

Adieu! I am truly Yours. I hope her hair is not red tho'.

I have been abroad, or I had wrote sooner.

To HORACE WALPOLE

[*Cambridge, December 30, 1764*].

I have received the C. of O.,[1] & return you my thanks for it. It engages our attention here, makes some of us cry a little, & all in general afraid to go to bed o' nights. We take it for a translation, & should believe it to be a true story, if it were not for St. Nicholas.

When your pen was in your hand, you might have been a little more communicative: for, tho' disposed enough to believe the

[1] The Castle of Otranto.

Opposition rather consumptive, I am entirely ignorant of all the symptoms. even what the Yorks have been doing for themselves, or attempting to do, is to me a secret. Your canonical book I have been reading with great satisfaction. He speaketh as one having authority. If Englishmen have any feeling left, methinks they must feel now; & if the Ministry have any feeling (whom no body will suspect of insensibilty) they must cut off the Author's ears, for it is in all the forms a most wicked libel. Is the old Man, & the Lawyer put on, or is it real? or has some real Lawyer furnish'd a good part of the materials, & another Person employ'd them? This I guess, for there is an uncouthness of diction in the beginning, which is not supported throughout, though it now & then occurs again, as if the Writer was weary of supporting the character he had assumed, when the subject had warmed him beyond dissimulation.

Rousseau's letters I am reading heavily, heavily! He justifies himself, till he convinces me, that he deserved to be burnt, at least that his book did. I am not got thro' him, & you never will. Voltaire I detest, & have not seen his book: I shall in good time. You surprise me, when you talk of going in February: pray, does all the Minority go too? I hope, you have a *reason. Desperare de republicâ* is a deadly sin in politicks.

Adieu! I will not take my leave of you, for (you perceive) this letter means to beg another, when you can spare a little.

To WILLIAM MASON

[*Cambridge, January 17, 1765*].

Dear Mr. Mason

As you are alone & not quite well, I do feel a little sort of (I am almost ashamed to speak it) tenderness for you: but then I comfort myself with the thought, that it does not proceed from any remnant of old inclination or kindness I have for you. That (you must allow) would be folly, as our places of abode are so distant, & our occupations & pursuits so different. But the true cause is, that I am pretty lonely too, & besides have a complaint in my eyes, that possibly may end in blindness. It consists in not being able to read at all with one eye, & having very often the *Muscæ Volitantes* before the other. I may be allow'd therefore to think a little of you (& Delaval) wihout any disparagement to my knowledge of Mankind & of human Nature.

The match you talk of is no more consummated than your own, & Kitty is still a Maid for the Doctor: so that he wants the *requisite* thing, & yet (I'll be sworn) his happiness is very little impair'd. I take broil'd Salmon to be a dish much more necessary at your table than his. I had heard in Town (as you have) that they were married; & long'd to go to Spilsby & make them a visit: but here I learn, it is not true yet, whatever it may be. I read & liked the Epigram as it was printed, & do insist, it is better without the last lines, not that the thought is amiss, but because the same rhyme is repeated, & the sting is not in the epigrammatic style: I mean, not easy & familiar. In a Satyr it might do very well. Mr. Churchill is dead indeed, drown'd in a butt of claret, which was tap'd on the meeting of the Friends at Boulogne: he made an excellent end, as his Executor Humphrey Cotes testifies. I did not write any of the elegies, being busy in writing the *Temple of Tragedy*. Send for it forthwith, for you are highly interested in it. If I had not own'd the thing, perhaps you might have gone, & taken it for the Revd. Mr. Langhorne's. It is divine!

I have not read the Philosophic Dictionary. I can stay with great patience for any thing that comes from Voltaire: they tell me it is frippery & blasphemy & wit. I could have forgiven myself, if I had not read Rousseau's letters. Always excepting the *Contract Social,* it is the dullest performance he ever publish'd. it is a weak attempt to separate the miracles from the morality of the Gospel: the latter (he would have you think) he believes, was sent from God, & the former he very explicitly takes for an imposture. This is in order to prove the cruelty & injustice of the State of Geneva in burning his Emile. The latter part of his book is to shew the abuses, that have crept into the constitution of his countrey, which point (if you are concerned about it) he makes out very well: and his intention in this is plainly to raise a tumult in the City, & to be revenged on the *Petit Conseil,* who condemn'd his writings to the flames.

Cambridge itself is fruitful enough of events to furnish out many paragraphs in my Gazette. The most important is, that Frog Walker is dead: his last words were (as the Nurses sate by him & said, ah, poor Gentleman, he is going!) Going, going, where am I a-going? I'm sure, I know no more than the Man in the moon! Dr. Ridlington has been given over with a dropsy these 10 weeks: he refused all tapping & scarifying, but obey'd other directions; till finding all was over, he prescribed to himself a boil'd chicken entire, & five quarts of small beer. After this he brought up great quantities of blood, the swelling & suffocation & all signs of water disappear'd. Every body has ceased to enquire after him, & as he would not die, when he should, they are resolved to proceed as if he were dead & buried. Dr. Newcome is dead: for 6 weeks or more before his death he was distracted, not childish, but really raving. For the last 3 weeks he took no nourishment but by force. Miss Kirke & the younger Beadon are Executors & residuary Legatees: I believe he left about 10,000£, but there are many legacies. had I a pen of adamant, I could not describe the business, the agitation, the tempest, the University is in about the Margaret Professorship. Only D. D.'s & B. D.'s have votes, so that there are acts upon acts: the bell is eternally tolling as in time of pestilence, & no body knows whose turn it may be next. the Candidates are Dr. Law, & Z. Brooke & my Lord Sandwich. the day is Saturday next. But alas! what is this to the warm region of St John's? it is like Lisbon on the day of the earthquake! it is like the fire of London! I can hear & smell it hither. Here too appears the furious Zachary, but his forces are but three or four men. Here towers Dr. Rutherforth, himself an Host, & he has about 3 champions. There Skinner with his powerful oratory, & the decent Mr. Alvis, with their several invisible squadrons. Ogden & Gunning each fighting for himself & disdaining the assistance of others. but see, where Frampton rages with his 17 votes, & on his buckler glitters the formidable name of Sandwich, at which Fiends tremble. last of all comes with his mines & counter-mines, & old Newcastle at his back, the irresistable force of Powell. 23 are a majority, & he has already 22 & ½. If it lapses to the Seniors, he has it. If it lapses to the Visitor, he has it. In short (as we all believe) he has it every way. I know you are overjoy'd, especially for that he has the Newcastle interest. I have had a very civil visit of two hours from [the] *Archimage,* busy as he is, for you know, I inherit all y[our] old acquaintance, as I do all Delaval's old distempers. I visited Dr. Balguy the other day at Winchester, & he me at Southampton: we are as great as two pease. The day of election at St John's is Friday-se'nnight.

Mr. Brown is well, & has forgot you. Mr. Nicholls is profuse of his thanks to me for your civilities to him at York, of which (God knows) I knew no more than the Man in the moon. Adieu!

To WILLIAM MASON

[*London. Nov. 8, 1765*].

Dear Mason

Res est sacra *miser* (says the Poet) but I say, it is the happy Man, that is the sacred thing; & therefore let the Profane keep their distance: he is one of Lucretius' Gods, supremely blest in the contemplation of his own felicity, & what has he to do with Worshippers? This (mind) is the first reason, why I did not come to York. The second is, that I do not love confinement, & probably by next summer may be permitted to *touch* whom & where & with what I think fit without giving you any offence. The third & last, & not the least perhaps, is, that the finances were at so low an ebb, that I could not exactly do what I wish'd, but was obliged to come the shortest road to Town & recruit them. I do not justly know what your taste in reasons may be, since you alter'd your condition; but there is the ingenious, the petulant, & the dull, for you. Any one would have done, for in my conscience I do not believe you care a half-penny for reasons at present. So God bless ye both, & give ye all ye wish, when ye are restored to the use of your wishes!

I am return'd from Scotland charm'd with my expedition: it is of the Highlands I speak: the Lowlands are worth seeing once, but the Mountains are extatic, & ought to be visited in pilgrimage once a year. None but those monstrous creatures of God know how to join so much beauty with so much horror. A fig for your Poets, Painters, Gardiners, & Clergymen,[1] that have not been among them: their imagination can be made up of nothing but bowling-greens, flowering shrubs, horse-ponds, Fleet-ditches, shell-grottoes, & Chinée-rails. Then I had so beautiful an autumn: Italy could hardly produce a nobler scene, or a finer season. And this so sweetly contrasted with that perfection of nastiness, & total want of accommodation, that Scotland only can supply. Oh! you would have bless'd yourself. I shall certainly go again. What a pity 'tis I can't draw, nor describe, nor ride on horseback!

Stonhewer is the busiest creature upon earth, except Mr. Fraser: they stand pretty tight for all his Royal Highness. Have you read (oh no! I had forgot) Dr. Lowth's pamphlet against your Uncle the Bishop? Oh how he works him! I hear he will soon be on the same bench. Today Mr. Hurd came to see me, but we had not a word of that matter: he is grown pure & plump, just of the proper breadth for a celebrated Town-Preacher. There was Dr. Balguy too: he says, Mrs. Mason is very handsome; so you are his Friend for ever. Lord Newnham (I hear) has ill health of late: it is a nervous case. & have a care! How do your eyes do? The hereditary Prince the morning after he was married, I remember, said to somebody, Sauf le respect que je dois a son Altesse Royale, jamais Princesse n'a eté mieux f—e. Can you in conscience mutatis mutandis say the same? I know any body can & will say the same: but can you say it verbo Sacerdotis? Adieu! My respects to the Bride. I would kiss her, but you stand by & pretend, it is not the fashion: tho' I know, they do so at Hull. I am

Ever Yours

T G:

---

[1] A hit at Mason, who was all four.

To THOMAS WHARTON

March 5, 1766. Pemb. C.

Dear Doctor

I am amazed at myself, when I think I have never wrote to you: to be sure it is the sin of witchcraft or something worse. Something indeed might be said for it, had I been married like Mason, who (for the first time since that great event) has just thought fit to tell me, that he never pass'd so happy a winter as the last, & this in spite of his anxieties, which perhaps (he says) might even make a part of his happiness: for his Wife is by no means in health, she has a constant cough, yet he is assured, her lungs are not affected, & that it is nothing of the consumptive kind. What say you to this case? May I flatter him, that breeding will be a cure for this disorder? If so, I hear she is in a fair way to be well. As to me I have been neither happy, nor miserable: but in a gentle stupefaction of mind, & very tolerable health of body hitherto. If they last, I shall not much complain. The accounts one has lately had from all parts make me suppose you buried under the snow, like the old Queen of Denmark: as soon as you are dug out, I should rejoice to hear your voice from the battlements of Old-Park. The greatest cold we have felt here was Jan. 2, Thermom. (in the garden) at 4 in the afternoon standing at 30 Deg. ½, and next day fell a little snow, which did not lie. It was the first we had had during the winter. Again, Feb. 5 toward night, Therm. was down at 30 D. with a clear sky; the snow-drops then beginning to blow in the garden: next day was a little snow. But on the 11th & 12th fell a deep snow (the weather not very cold) which however was melted on ye 15th, & made a flood in the river. Next day the Thrush was singing & the Rooks building. At & about London instead of snow they had heavy rains. On the 19th the red Hepatica blew, & next day the Primrose. The Crocus is now in full bloom. So ends my chronicle.

My oracle of state (who now & then utters a little, as far as he may with discretion) is a very slave & pack-horse, that never breaths any air better than that of London, except like an Apprentice, on Sundays with his Master and Co. However he is in health, & a very good Boy. It is strange, the turn that things have taken. That the late Ministry should negociate a reconciliation with Lord B., & that Lord Temple should join them; that they should after making their (bad) apologies be received with a gracious kind of contempt, & told that his Lordship could enter into no political connections with them: that on the first division on the American business that happen'd in the H. of Lords they should however all join to carry a point against the Ministry by a majority indeed of four only, but the D. of Y—k present & making one: that when the Ministers expostulated in a proper place, they should be seriously assured the K. would support them. That on a division on an insignificant point to try their strength in the H. of Commons they should again lose it by 12 majority: that they should persist nevertheless: that Mr. Pitt should appear *tanquam e machinâ,* speak for 3 hours & ½, & assert the rights of the Colonies in their greatest latitude: that the Minister should profess himself ready to act with & even serve under him: that he should receive such a compliment with coldness, & a sort of derision: that Norton should move to send him to the Tower: that when the great questions came on, the Ministry should always carry their point at one, two, three in the morning by majorities of 110 & 170 (Mr. Pitt entirely concurring with them, & the Tories, People of the Court, & many Placemen, even Lord G. Sackville, constantly voting against them) all these events are unaccountable on any principles of common-sense. I attribute much of the singular part to the interposition of *Women* as rash as they are foolish. On Monday (I do not doubt, tho' as yet I do not certainly know it) the Bill to repeal the Stamp-act went thro' that House, & to-day it is before the Lords, who surely will not venture to throw it out. oh, that they would!—but after this important business is well over, there must be an eclaircissement: some amends must be made & some gracious condescensions insisted on, or else who would go on, that really means to serve his country! The D. of Bedford & Lord Temple were gone down to their Villas, & I believe are not likely to come back. Lord Chesterfield, who had not been for many years at the house, came the other day to qualify himself in order to leave a proxy, that should vote with the Ministry. Some body (I thought) made no bad application of those lines in Virgil L. 6, v. 489

At Danaum proceres, Agamemnoniæq phalanges &c.

to Mr. Pitt's first appearance (for no one expected him) in the house. Turn to the place.

Every thing is politicks. There are no literary productions worth your notice, at least of our country. The French have finish'd their great Encyclopedie in 17 Volumes: but there are many flimsey articles very hastily treated, & great incorrectness of the Press. There are now 13 Vol. of Buffon's Natural History, & he is not come to the Monkies yet, who are a very numerous people. The Life of Petrarch has entertain'd me: it is not well written, but very curious & laid together from his own letters & the original writings of the 14th Century: so that it takes in much of the history of those obscure times, & the characters of many remarkable persons. There are 2 vols. 4to, & another (unpublish'd yet) that will compleat it.

Mr. W. writes me now & then a long and lively letter from Paris, to which place he went last summer with the gout upon him sometimes in his limbs, often in his stomach & head. He has got somehow well (not by means of the climate, one would think) goes to all publick places, sees all the best company & is very much in fashion. He says, he sunk like Queen Eleanour at Charing-Cross, & has risen again at Paris. He returns again in April: but his health is certainly in a deplorable state. Mad. de la Perriere is come over from the Hague to be Ministress at London. Her Father-in-law Viry is now first Minister at Turin. I sate a morning with her before I left London. She is a prodigious fine Lady, & a Catholick (tho she did not expressly own it to me) not fatter than she was: she had a cage of foreign birds & a piping Bullfinch at her elbow,. two little Dogs on a cushion in her lap, a Cockatoo on her shoulder, & a sl[ight] suspicion of Rouge on her cheeks. They were all exceeding glad to [see] me, & I them.

Pray tell me the history of your winter, & present my respects to Mrs. Wharton. I hope Miss Wharton & Miss Peggy with the assistance of Sister Betty make a great progress in Natural History: recommend me to all their good graces, & believe me ever

Truly Yours

If you chance to see or send to Mr. & Mrs. Leighton, I will trouble you to make my compliments: I have never received the box of shells, tho' possibly it may wait for me at Mr. Jonathan's in Town, where I shall be in April. Mr. Brown is well & desires to be remember'd to you and Mrs. Wharton. I have just heard, there are like to be warm debates in the house of Lords, but that the Ministry will undoubtedly carry it[1] in spite of them all. They say, Lord Cambden will soon be Chancellour.

To NORTON NICHOLLS

Aug. 26, 1766, Pemb. Hall.

Dear Sir

It is long since that I heard you were gone in hast into Yorkshire on account of your Mother's illness, & the same letter inform'd me, that she was recover'd. Otherwise I had then wrote to you only to beg you would take care of her, & to inform you, that I had discover'd a thing very little known, which is, that in one's whole life one never can have any more than a single Mother. You may think this is obvious, & (what you call) a trite observation. You are a green Gossling! I was at the same age (very near) as wise as you, & yet I never discover'd this (with full evidence & conviction, I mean) till it was too late. It is 13 years ago, & seems but yesterday, & every day I live it sinks deeper into my heart. Many a corollary could I draw from this axiom for your use (not for my own) but I will leave you the

[1] The Repeal of the Stamp Act.

merit of doing it yourself. Pray, tell me how your own health is. I conclude it perfect, as I hear you offer'd yourself for a guide to Mr. Palgrave into the Sierra-Morena of Yorkshire. For me I pass'd the end of May & all June in Kent not disagreeably. The country is all a garden, gay, rich, & fruitfull, & (from the rainy season) had preserved, till I left it, all that emerald verdure, which commonly one only sees for the first fortnight of the spring. In the west part of it from every eminence the eye catches some long winding reach of the Thames or Medway with all their navigation. in the east the sea breaks in upon you, & mixes its white transient sails & glittering blew expanse with the deeper & brighter greens of the woods & corn. This last sentence is so fine I am quite ashamed. But no matter! you must translate it into prose. Palgrave, if he heard it, would cover his face with his pudding-sleeve. I went to Margate for a day: one would think, it was Bartholomew Fair that had *flown* down: From Smithfield to Kent in the London machine like my Lady Stuffdamask (to be sure you have read the New Bath Guide, the most fashionable of books) so then I did *not* go to Kingsgate, because it belong'd to my Lord Holland: but to Ramsgate I did, & so to Sandwich & Deal & Dover & Folkstone & Hithe all along the coast very delightful. I do not tell you of the great & small beasts & creeping things innumerable that I met with, because you do not suspect, that this world is inhabited by any thing but Men & Women, & Clergy, & such two-legged cattle. Now I am here again very disconsolate & all alone: even Mr. Brown is gone, & the cares of this world are coming thick upon me, I do not mean Children. You I hope are better off, riding & walking with Mr. Aislaby, singing Duets with my Cousin Fanny, improving with Mr. Weddell, conversing with Mr. Harry Duncomb. I must not wish for you here: besides I am going to Town at Michaelmas, by no means for amusement. Do you remember, how we are to go into Wales next year? well!—Adieu, I am

Sincerely Yours,

T G:

Pray how does poor Temple find himself in his new situation? is Lord L. as good as his letters were? what is come of the Father & Brother? Have you seen Mason?

To THOMAS WHARTON

[*Cambridge, August 26, 1766*].

Dear Doctor

Whatever my pen may do, I am sure my thoughts expatiate no where oftener or with more pleasure than to Old-Park. I hope you have made my peace with Miss Debo. It is certain, whether her name were in my letter or not, she was as present to my memory, as the rest of the little family, & I desire you would present her with two kisses in my name, & one apiece to all the others: for I shall take the liberty to kiss them all (great & small) as you are to be my proxy.

In spite of the rain, which I think continued with very short intervals till the beginning of this month, & quite effaced the summer from the year, I made shift to pass May & June not disagreeably in Kent. I was surprised at the beauty of the road to Canterbury, which (I know not why) had not struck me in the same manner before. the whole county is a rich & well-cultivated garden, orchards, cherry-grounds, hop-gardens, intermix'd with corn & frequent villages, gentle risings cover'd with wood, and every where the Thames & Medway breaking in upon the Landscape with all their navigation. it was indeed owing to the bad weather, that the whole scene was dress'd in that tender emerald-green, which one usually sees only for a fortnight in the opening of spring, & this continued till I left the country. my residence was eight miles east of Canterbury in a little quiet valley on the skirts of Barham-down. In these parts the whole soil is chalk, and whenever it holds up, in half an hour it is dry enough to walk out. I took the opportunity of three or four days fine weather to go into the Isle of Thanet, saw Margate (which is Bartholomew-Fair by the seaside) Ramsgate, & other places there, & so came by Sandwich, Deal, Dover, Folkstone, & Hithe back again. The coast is not like Hartlepool: there are no rocks, but only chalky cliffs of no great height, till you come to Dover. There indeed they are noble & picturesque, & the opposite coasts of France begin to bound your view, which was left before to range unlimited by any thing but the horizon: yet it is by no means a *shipless* sea, but every where peopled with white sails & vessels of all sizes in motion; and take notice (except in the Isle, which is all corn-fields, & has very little inclosure) there are in all places hedge-rows & tall trees even within a few yards of the beach, particularly Hithe stands on an eminence cover'd with wood. I shall confess we had fires of a night (ay, & a day too) several times even in June: but don't go & take advantage of this, for it was the most untoward year that ever I remember.

Your Friend Rousseau (I doubt) grows tired of Mr. Davenport & Derbyshire. He has pick'd a quarrel with David Hume & writes him letter of 14 pages Folio upbraiding him with all his *noirceurs*. Take one only as a specimen, he says, that at Calais they chanced to sleep in the same room together, & that he overheard David talking in his sleep, & saying, *Ah! Je le tiens, ce Jean-Jacques lá.* In short (I fear) for want of persecution & admiration (for these are his real complaints) he will go back to the continent.

What shall I say to you about the Ministry? I am as angry as a Common-council Man of London about my Lord Chatham: but a little more patient, & will hold my tongue till the end of the year. In the mean time I do mutter in secret & to you, that to quit the house of Commons, his natural strength; to sap his own popularity & grandeur (which no one but himself could have done) by assuming a foolish title; & to hope that he could win by it & attach to him a Court, that hate him, & will dismiss him, as soon as ever they dare, was the weakest thing, that ever was done by so great a Man. Had it not been for this, I should have rejoiced at the breach between him & Lord Temple, & at the union between him & the D. of Grafton & Mr. Conway: but patience! we shall see! St. perhaps is in the country (for he hoped for a month's leave of absence) & if you see him, you will learn more than I can tell you.

Mason is at Aston. He is no longer so anxious about his Wife's health, as he was, tho' I find she still has a cough, & moreover I find she is not with child: but he made such a bragging, how could one chuse but believe him.

When I was in town, I mark'd in my pocket-book the utmost limits & division of the two columns in your Thermometer, & ask'd Mr. Ayscough the Instrument-Maker on Ludgate Hill, what scales they were. He immediately assured me, that one was Fahrenheit's, & shew'd me one exactly so divided. The other he took for Reaumur's but, as he said there were different scales of his contrivance, he could not exactly tell, which of them it was. Your Brother told me, you wanted to know, who wrote Duke Wharton's Life in the Biography: I think, it is chiefly borrowed from a silly book enough call'd *Memoirs of that Duke*: but who put it together there, no one can inform me. The only person certainly known to write in that vile collection (I mean these latter volumes) is Dr. Nicholls, who was expell'd here for stealing books.

Have you read the *New Bath-Guide?* It is the only [thing] in fashion, & is a new & original kind of humour. Miss Prue's Conversion I doubt you will paste down, as Sir W. St. Quintyn did, before he carried it to his daughter. Yet I remember you all read *Crazy Tales* without pasting. Buffon's first collection of Monkies are come out (it makes the 14th volume) something, but not much, to my edification: for he is pretty well acquainted with their persons, but not with their manners.

I shall be glad to hear, how far Mrs. Ettrick has succeeded, & when you see an end to her troubles. My best respects to Mrs. Wharton, & compliments to all your family: I will not name them, least I should affront any body. Adieu, dear Sir,

I am most sincerely Yours,

T G:

Mr. Brown is gone to see his Brother near Margate. When is Lord Str. to be married? If Mr. & Mrs. Jonathan are with you, I desire my compliments.

To WILLIAM MASON

5 Oct. 1766. P. Hall.

Dear Mason

I was going to write to you, when I received your letter, and on the same subject.[1] The first news I had was from Stonhewer on the 23d. of Sept. in these words:

'This morning Dr. B. dispatch'd himself: he had been for several days past very low-spirited, & within the last two or three talk'd of the necessity of dying in such a manner as to alarm the people about him: they removed as they thought every thing, that might serve his purpose. But he had contrived to get at a razor unknown to them, & took the advantage of a minute's absence of his servants to make use of it.' I wrote to him again (I suspect, he knows our secret,[2] tho' not from me) to make farther enquiries, & he says, 27 Sept., 'I have tried to find out, whether there was any appearance or cause of discontent in B., but can hear of none. A bodily complaint of the gouty kind, that fell upon his nerves & affected his spirits in a very great degree is all that I can get any information of; & I am told besides, that he was some years ago in the same dejected way, & under the care of *proper attendants*.' Mr. W. too in answer to a letter I had written to enquire after his health after giving an account of himself, while under the care of Pringle, adds, 'He (Pringle) had another Patient at the same time, who has ended very unhappily, that poor Dr. B. The unfortunate Man apprehended himself going mad, & two nights after cut his throat in bed.' This is all I know at present of the matter. I have told it you literally, & I conceal nothing. As I go to town tomorrow, if I learn any thing more, you shall soon hear from me. In the mean time I think we may fairly conclude, that if he had had

---

[1] The subject was the suicide of Dr. John Brown on 23 Sept. The receipt of the news of his death had evidently caused much concern to both Mason and Gray, who feared that Mason's recently published satire, *Ode on John Brown,* might have been a contributory cause to his suicide.

[2] 'Our secret' was that Mason was the author of the *Ode on John Brown.*

any other cause added to his constitutional infirmity, it would have been uppermost in his mind: he would have talk'd or raved about it, & the first thing we should have heard of, would have been this, which (I do assure you) I have never heard from any body. There is in this neighbourhood a Mr. Wale, who once was in the Russia-trade & married a Woman of that country: he always maintain'd, that Dr. B. would never go thither, whatever he might pretend; & that tho' fond of the glory of being invited thither, he would certainly find or make a pretence for staying at home. Very possibly therefore he might have engaged himself so far, that he knew not how to draw back with honour; or might have received rough words from the Russian Minister offended with his prevarication. This supposition is at least as likely as yours; added to what I have said before, much more so: if it be necessary to suppose any other cause than the lunatick disposition of the Man. And yet I will not disguise to you, that I felt as you do on the first news of this sad accident, & had the same uneasy ideas about it.

I am sorry the cause you mention should be the occasion of your coming to London: tho' perhaps change of air may do more than medicine. In this length of time I should think you must be fully apprised, whether her looks or strength or embonpoint have suffer'd by this cough: if not; surely there is no real danger. Yet I do not wonder, she should wish to get rid of so troublesome a companion.

When I can meet with the book, I will transcribe what you mention from *Mallet*. I shall write again soon. Do you know of any great, or at least rich, family that want a young Man worth his weight in gold to take care of their eldest hope. If you do, remember I have such a one, or shall have (I fear) shortly to sell: but they must not stand haggling about him, & besides they must be very good sort of people too, or they shall not have him. Adieu! My respects to Mrs. Mason. I am ever

Sincerely Yours.

Mr. Brown desires his best compliments to you both.

To JAMES BROWN

18 Nov. 1766. Jermyn-Street.

Dear Sir

I paid the sum abovemention'd this morning at Gillam's Office in Bishopsgate-Street: the remittance you will please to pay out of it. I have not time to add all the bad news of the times, but in a few days you shall have some of it; tho' the worst of all is just what I can not write. I am perfectly out of humour, & so will you be.

Mason is here, & has brought his Wife, a pretty, modest, innocent, interesting figure, looking like 18, tho' she is near 28. she does not speak, only whispers, & her cough as troublesome as ever: yet I have great hopes, there is nothing consumptive. she is strong & in good spirits. We were all at the Opera together on Saturday last. They desire their loves to you. I have seen Mr. Talbot, & Delaval lately. Adieu! I am ever

Yours
T G:

I can not find Mons. de la Chalotais in any of the shops. Lord St. I am told is to be married here. I know nothing of Pa., but that he was still at Mr. Weddell's a fortnight since. Be so good to tell me you have recieved this (if you can) by the return of the Post.

To WILLIAM MASON

Jan. 27, 1767. Pemb. Hall.

Dear Mason

Dr. Swift says, one never should write to one's Friends but in high health & spirits. By the way it is the last thing people in those circumstances usually think of doing: but it is sure, if I were to wait for them, I never should write at all. At present I have had for these six weeks a something growing in my throat, which nothing does any service to, & which will, I suppose, in due time stop up the passage. I go however about, & the pain is very little. You will say perhaps, the malady is as little, & the stoppage is in the imagination. No matter for that! if it is not sufficient to prove want of health (for indeed this is all I ail) it is so much the stronger proof of the want of spirits. So take it as you please, I carry my point, & shew you, that it is very obliging in me to write at all. Indeed perhaps on your account, I should not have done it: but after three such weeks of Lapland-weather I can not but enquire after Mrs. Mason's health. If she has withstood such a winter & her cough never the worse: she may defy the Doctors & all their works. pray, tell me how she is, for I interest myself for her not merely on your account, but on her own. These three last mornings have been very vernal & mild: has she tasted the air of the new year at least in Hyde-Park?

Mr. Brown will wait on her next week, & touch her. He has been confined to lie on a couch, & under the Surgeon's hands eversince the first of January with a broken shin ill-doctor'd. he is just now got abroad, & obliged to come to Town about Monday on *particular* business.

Stonhewer was so kind as to tell me the mystery now accomplish'd, before I received your letter. I rejoice in all his accessions: I wish, you would persuade him to take unto him a Wife: but don't let her be a fine Lady. Adieu. Present my respects & good wishes to Argentile. I am truly

Yours
T G

To WILLIAM MASON

March 28. 1767.

My Dear Mason

I break in upon you at the moment, when we least of all are permitted to disturb our Friends, only to say, that you are daily & hourly present to my thoughts. If the *worst* be not yet past: you will neglect & pardon me. But if the last struggle be over: if the poor object of your long anxieties be no longer sensible to your kindness, or to her own sufferings: allow me (at least in idea, for what could I do, were I present, more than this?) to sit by you in silence, & pity from my heart not her, who is at rest; but you, who lose her. May He, who made us, the Master of our pleasures, & of our pains, preserve & support you! Adieu

I have long understood, how little you had to hope.

To JAMES BROWN

[*Jermyn Street, c. May 28, 1767*].

How do you do, good Mr. Brown? Do your inclinations begin to draw northward, as mine do, and may I take you a place soon? I wait but for an answer from Mason how to regulate our journey, which I should hope may take place in a little more than a week. I shall write a line again to settle the exact day, but you may now tell me whether you will come to town, or be taken up at Buckden, or thirdly, whether you will go in a chaise with me by short journeys, and see places in our way. I dined yesterday on Richmond Hill, after seeing Chiswick, and Strawberry, and Sion; and be assured the face of the country looks an emerald, if you love jewels.

The Westminster Theatre is like to come to a sudden end. The manager will soon embark for Italy without Callista. The reason is a speech, which his success in Lothario emboldened him to make the other day in a greater theatre. It was on the subject of America, and added so much strength to the opposition, that they came within six of the majority. He did not vote, however, though his two brothers did, and, like good boys, with the ministry. For this he has been rattled on both sides of his ears, and forbid to appear there any more. The Houses wait with impatience the conclusion of the East India business to rise. The E. of Chatham is mending slowly in his health, but sees nobody on business yet, nor has he since he came from Marlborough: yet he goes out daily for an airing.

I have seen his lordship of Cloyne often. He is very jolly, and we devoured four raspberry-puffs together in Cranbourn-alley standing at a pastrycook's shop in the street; but he is gone, and Heaven knows when we shall eat any more.

Rousseau you see is gone too. I read his letter to my Lord Chancellor from Spalding, and hear he has written another long one to Mr. Conway from Dover, begging he might no longer be detained here. He retains his pension. The whole seems madness increasing upon him. There is a most bitter satire on him and his Madlle. le Vassiur, written by Voltaire, and called *Guerre de Geneve*. Adieu, and let me hear from you.

I am ever yours,

T. G.

How do our Elmsted friends? Are they married yet? Old Pa. is here, and talks of writing soon to you.

To JAMES DODSLEY

[*c. Feb. 1, 1768*].

Let the Title be only *Poems by Mr. Gray* without any mention of notes or additions. You will judge, whether what few notes there are should stand at bottom of each page, or be thrown to the end. All I desire is, that the text be accurately printed, & therefore whoever corrects the press, should have some acquaintance with the Greek, Latin, & Italian, as well as the English, tongues. Let the order stand thus, unless you have begun to print already: if so, it is indifferent to me.

1. Ode. (Lo, where the rosy-bosom'd &c.)
2. Ode, on the death of a favourite Cat.
3. Ode, on a distant prospect of Eton-College.
4. Ode, to Adversity.
5. The progress of Poësy, a Pindaric Ode.
6. The Bard, a Pindaric Ode.
7. The Fatal Sisters.
8. The Descent of Odin.
9. The Triumphs of Owen, a fragment.
10. Elegy, written in a country church-yard.

You will print the four first & the last from your own large edition (first publish'd with Mr. B.'s plates) in the 5th & 6th you will do well to follow the edition printed at St.y-hill: I mention this, because there are several little faults of the press in your Miscellanies. Remember, the *Long Story* must be quite omitted. now for the notes.

[Here follow the notes and the text and notes of Poems 7, 8, 9.]

I hope, you have not begun to reprint: but if you have, you must throw the notes, &c. to the end, or where you please, omitting the mottoes, which do not much signify. When you have done, I shall desire you to present in my name a copy to Mr. Walpole in Arlington-street, another to Mr. Daines Barrington (he is one of the Welch Judges) in the Inner-Temple; & a third to Mr. *F. Bulter at Andover*: whether this latter Gentleman be living or not, or in that neighbourhood, I am ignorant: but you will oblige me in making the enquiry. If you have no better means of knowing, a line directed to the Post-mistress at Andover will bring you information. After this you may (if you please) bestow another copy or two on me. I am

Your obedt. humble Servant

T. Gray.

P. S. It is Mr. *Foulis of Glasgow,* that prints them in Scotland: he has been told, that you are doing the same. I have desired, he would not print a great number, & could wish the same of you.

To HORACE WALPOLE

Feb. 14, 1768. Pembroke College.

I received the book[1] you were so good to send me, and have read it again (indeed I could hardly be said to have read it before) with attention and with pleasure. Your second edition is so rapid in its progress, that it will now hardly answer any purpose to tell you either my own objections, or those of other people. Certain it is, that you are universally read here; but what *we* think, is not

[1] Walpole's *Historic Doubts on the Life and Reign of King Richard the Third.*

so easy to come at. We stay as usual to see the success, to learn the judgment of the town, to be directed in our opinions by those of more competent judges. If they like you, we shall; if any one of name write against you, we give you up: for we are modest and diffident of ourselves, and not without reason. History in particular is not our *fort;* for (the truth is) we read only modern books and the pamphlets of the day. I have heard it objected, that you raise doubts and difficulties, and do not satisfy them by telling us what was *really* the case. I have heard you charged with disrespect to the king of Prussia; and above all to king William, and the revolution. These are seriously the most sensible things I have heard said, and all that I recollect. If you please to justify yourself, you may.

My own objections are little more essential: they relate chiefly to inaccuracies of style, which either debase the expression or obscure the meaning. I could point out several small particulars of this kind, and will do so, if you think it can serve any purpose after publication. When I hear you read, they often escape me, partly because I am attending to the subject, and partly because from habit I understand you where a stranger might often be at a loss.

As to your arguments, most of the principal parts are made out with a clearness and evidence that no one would expect where materials are so scarce. Yet I still suspect Richard of the murder of Henry VI. The chronicler of Croyland charges it full on him, though without a name or any mention of circumstances. The interests of Edward were the interests of Richard too, though the throne were not then in view; and that Henry still stood in their way, they might well imagine, because, though deposed and imprisoned once before, he had regained his liberty, and his crown; and was still adored by the people. I should think, from the word *tyranni,* the passage was written after Richard had assumed the crown: but, if it was earlier, does not the bare imputation imply very early suspicions at least of Richard's bloody nature, especially in the mouth of a person that was no enemy to the house of York, nor friend to that of Beaufort?

That the duchess of Burgundy, to try the temper of the nation, should set up a false pretender to the throne (when she had the true duke of York in her hands), and that the queen-mother (knowing her son was alive) should countenance that design, is a piece of policy utterly incomprehensible; being the most likely means to ruin their own scheme, and throw a just suspicion of fraud and falsehood on the cause of truth, which Henry could not fail to seize and turn to his own advantage.

Mr. Hume's first query, as far as relates to the queen-mother, will still have some weight. Is it probable, she should give her eldest daughter to Henry, and invite him to claim the crown, unless she had been sure that her sons were then dead? As to her seeming consent to the match between Elizabeth and Richard, she and her daughters were in his power, which appeared now well fixed, his enemies' designs within the kingdom being every where defeated, and Henry unable to raise any considerable force abroad. She was timorous and hopeless; or she might dissemble, in order to cover her secret dealings with Richmond: and if this were the case, she hazarded little, supposing Richard to dissemble too, and never to have thought seriously of marrying his niece.

Another unaccountable thing is, that Richard, a prince of the house of York, undoubtedly brave, clear-sighted, artful, attentive to business; of boundless generosity, as appears from his grants; just and merciful, as his laws and his pardons seem to testify; having subdued the queen and her hated faction, and been called first to the protectorship and then to the crown by the body of the nobility and by the parliament; with the common people to friend (as Carte often asserts), and having nothing against him but the illegitimate family of his brother Edward, and the attainted house of Clarence (both of them within his power);—that such a man should see within a few months Buckingham, his best friend, and almost all the southern and western counties on one day in arms against him; that, having seen all these insurrections come to nothing, he should march with a gallant army against a handful of needy adventurers, led by a fugitive, who had not the shadow of a title, nor any virtues to recommend him, nor any foreign strength to depend on; that he should be betrayed by almost all his troops, and fall a sacrifice;—all this is to me utterly improbable, and I do not ever expect to see it accounted for.

I take this opportunity to tell you, that Algarotti (as I see in the new edition of his works printed at Leghorn) being employed to buy pictures for the king of Poland, purchased among others the famous Holbein, that was at Venice. It don't appear that he knew any thing of your book: yet he calls it *the consul Meyer and his family,* as if it were then known to be so in that city.

A young man here, who is a diligent reader of books, an antiquary, and a painter, informs me, that at the Red-lion inn at Newmarket is a piece of tapestry containing the very design of your marriage of Henry the sixth, only with several more figures in it, both men and women; that he would have bought it of the people, but they refused to part with it.

Mr. Mason, who is here, desires to present his respects to you. He says, that to efface from our annals the history of any tyrant is to do an essential injury to mankind: but he forgives it, because you have shown Henry the seventh to be a greater devil than Richard.

Pray do not be out of humour. When you first commenced an author, you exposed yourself to pit, box and gallery. Any coxcomb in the world may come in and hiss, if he pleases; aye, and (what is almost as bad) clap too, and you cannot hinder him. I saw a little squib fired at you in a newspaper by some of the *house of York,* for speaking lightly of chancellors. Adieu!

I am ever yours,

T. Gray.

To HORACE WALPOLE

Pembroke-college, Feb. 25, 1768.

To your friendly accusation, I am glad I can plead not guilty with a safe conscience. Dodsley told me in the spring that the plates from Mr. Bentley's designs were worn out, and he wanted to have them copied and reduced to a smaller scale for a new edition. I dissuaded him from so silly an expense, and desired he would put in no ornaments at all. The *Long Story* was to be totally omitted, as its only use (that of explaining the prints) was gone: but to supply the place of it in bulk, lest *my works* should be mistaken for the works of a flea, or a pismire, I promised to send him an equal weight of poetry or prose: so, since my return hither, I put up about two ounces of stuff; viz. The Fatal Sisters, The Descent of Odin(of both which you have copies), a bit of something from the Welch, and certain little notes, partly from justice (to acknowledge the debt, where I had borrowed any thing), partly from ill temper, just to tell the gentle reader, that Edward I. was not Oliver Cromwell, nor queen Elizabeth the witch of Endor. This is literally all; and with all this I shall be but a shrimp of an author. I gave leave also to print the same thing at Glasgow; but I doubt my packet has miscarried, for I hear nothing of its arrival as yet. To what you say to me so civilly, that I ought to write more, I reply in your own words (like the pamphleteer, who is going to confute you out of your own mouth), What has one to do, when *turned of fifty,* but really to think of finishing? However, I will be candid (for you seem to be so with me), and avow to you, that till fourscore-and-ten, whenever the humour takes me, I will write, because I like it; and because I like myself better when I do so. If I do not write much, it is because I cannot. As you have not this last plea, I see no reason why you should not continue as long as it is agreeable to yourself, and to all such as have any curiosity of judgment in the subjects you choose to treat. By the way let me tell you(while it is fresh) that lord Sandwich, who was lately dining at Cambridge, speaking (as I am told) handsomely of your book, said, it was pity you did not know that his cousin Manchester had a genealogy of the kings, which came down no lower than to Richard III. and at the end of it were two portraits of Richard and his son, in which that king appeared to be a handsome man. I tell you it as I heard it: perhaps you may think it worth enquiring into.

I have looked into Speed and Leslie. It appears very odd, that Speed in the speech he makes for P. Warbeck, addressed to James IV. of Scotland, should three times cite the *manuscript proclamation* of Perkin, then in the hands of Sir Robert Cotton; and yet when he gives us the proclamation afterwards (on occasion of the insurrection in Cornwall) he does not cite any such manuscript. In Casley's Catalogue of the Cotton Library you may see whether this manuscript proclamation still exists or not: if it does, it may be found at the Musæum. Leslie will give you no satisfaction at all: though no subject of England, he could not write freely on this matter, as the title of Mary his mistress to the crown of England was derived from that of Henry VII. Accordingly, he every where treats Perkin as an imposter; yet drops several little expressions inconsistent with that supposition. He has preserved no proclamation: he only puts a short speech into Perkin's mouth, the substance of which is taken by Speed, and translated in the end of his, which is a good deal longer: the whole matter is treated by Leslie very concisely and superficially. I can easily transcribe it, if you please; but I do not see that it could answer any purpose.

Mr. Boswell's book I was going to recommend to you, when I received your letter: it has pleased and moved me strangely, all (I mean) that relates to Paoli. He is a man born two thousand years after his time! The pamphlet proves what I have always maintained, that any fool may write a most valuable book by chance, if he will only tell us what he heard and saw with veracity. Of Mr. Boswell's truth I have not the least suspicion, because I am sure he could invent nothing of this kind. The true title of this part of his work is, A Dialogue between a Greengoose and a Hero.

I had been told of a manuscript in Benet-library: the inscription of it is *Itinerarium Fratris Simonis Simeonis et Hugonis Illuminatoris,* 1322. Would not one think this should promise something? They were two Franciscan friars that came from Ireland, and passed through Wales to London, to Canterbury, to Dover, and so to France in their way to Jerusalem. All that relates to our own country has been transcribed for me, and (sorry am I to say) signifies not a halfpenny: only this little bit might be inserted in your next edition of the Painters: Ad aliud caput civitatis (Londoniæ) est monasterium nigrorum monachorum nomine Westmonasterium, in quo constanter et communiter omnes reges Angliæ sepeliuntur——et eidem monasterio quasi immediatè conjungitur illud famosissimum palatium regis, in quo est illa vulgata camera, in cujus parietibus sunt omnes historiæ bellicæ totius Bibliæ ineffabiliter depictæ, atque in Gallico completissimè et perfectissimè conscriptæ, in non modicâ intuentium admiratione et maximâ regali magnificentiâ.

I have had certain observations on your Royal and Noble Authors given me to send you perhaps about three years ago: last week I found them in a drawer, and (my conscience being troubled) now enclose them to you. I have even forgot whose they are.

I have been also told of a passage in Ph. de Comines, which (if you know) ought not to have been passed over. The book is not at hand at present, and I must conclude my letter. Adieu!

I am ever yours,

T. Gray.

To the DUKE OF GRAFTON

Cambridge, July [*27 or 28*], *1768.*

My Lord,

Your Grace has dealt nobly with me; and the same delicacy of mind that induced you to confer this favour on me, unsolicited and unexpected, may perhaps make you averse to receive my sincerest thanks and grateful acknowledgments. Yet your Grace must excuse me, they will have their way: they are indeed but words; yet I know and feel they come from my heart, and therefore are not wholly unworthy of your Grace's acceptance. I even flatter myself (such is my pride) that you have some little satisfaction in your own work. If I did not deceive myself in this, it would compleat the happiness of,

My Lord,

Your Grace's

Most obliged and devoted servant.

To THOMAS WHARTON

Jermyn-Street. 1. Aug. (at Mr. Robert's) 1768.

Dear Doctor

I have been remiss in answering your last letter, which was sent me to Ramsgate from Cambridge: for I have passed a good part of the summer in different parts of Kent much to my satisfaction. Could I have advised any thing essential in poor Mrs. Ett.s case, I had certainly replied immediately: but we seem of one mind in it. There was nothing left but to appeal to Delegates (let the trouble & expence be what they will almost) & to punish, if it be practicable, that old Villain, who upon the bench of justice dared to set at nought all common sense & all humanity.

I write to you now chiefly to tell you (and I think you will be pleased, (nay, I expect the whole family will be pleased with it,) that on Sunday se'nnight, Brockett died by a fall from his horse, being(as I hear) drunk, & some say, returning from Hinchinbroke: that on the Wednesday following, I received a letter from the D. of Grafton, saying, He had the K.'s commands to *offer* me the vacant Professorship, that &c. (but I shall not write all he says) & he adds at the end, *that from private as well as publick considerations He must take the warmest part in approving so well judged a measure as he hopes I do not doubt of the real regard & esteem with which he has the honor to be,* &c. There's for you. So on Thursday the K. sign'd the warrant, & next day at his Levee I kiss'd his hand. He made me several gracious speeches. which I shall not report, because every body, who goes to court, does so. By the way I desire, you would say, that all the Cabinet-Council in words of great favour approved the nomination of your humble Servt. & this I am bid to say, & was told to leave my name at their several doors. I have told you the outside of the matter & all the manner: for the inside you know enough easily to guess it, & you will guess right. As to his Grace I have not seen him before or since.

I shall continue here perhaps a fortnight longer, perishing with heat: I have no Thermometer with me, but I feel it as I did at Naples. Next summer (if it be as much in my power, as it is in my wishes) I meet you at the foot of Skiddaw. My respects to Mrs. Wharton, & the young Ladies great & small: love to Robin & Richard. Adieu! I am truly

Yours.

At your instance I have kiss'd Mrs. Forster, & forgot old quarrels. I went to visit the Daughter, who has been brought to bed of a Boy, & there I met with the Mother.

To NORTON NICHOLLS

3 Aug. 1768. Jermyn-Street (*Mr. Roberts's.*)

Dear Sir

That Mr. Brockett has broke his neck, you will have seen in the News-papers; & also that I (your humble Servant) have kiss'd the K.'s hand for his succession. They both are true, but the manner how you know not; only I can assure you, that I had no hand at all in his fall, & *almost* as little in the second happy event. He died on the Sunday, on Wednesday following, his Gr. of Grafton wrote me a very polite letter to say, that his Maj. had commanded him to *offer* me the vacant Proessorship, not only as a reward of &c. but as a credit to &c. with much more too high for me to transcribe. *You are to say,* that I owe my nomination to the *whole Cabinet-Council,* & my success to the K.'s *particular knowledge of me.* This last he told me himself, tho' the day was so hot & the ceremony so embarrassing to me, that I hardly know what he said.

I am commission'd to make you an offer, which, I have told him (not the King) you would not accept, long ago. Mr. Barrett (whom you know) offers to you 100£ a-year with meat, drink, washing, chaise, & lodging, if you will please to accompany him thro' France into Italy. He has taken such a fancy to you, that

I can not but do what he desires me, being pleased with him for it. I know, it will never do, tho' before you grew a rich fat Rector, I have often wish'd (ay, & fish'd too) for such an opportunity. No matter! I desire you to write your answer to him yourself as civil, as you think fit, & then let me know the result. That's all. He lives at *Lee near Canterbury.*

Adieu! I am to perish here with heat this fortnight yet, & then to Cambridge. Dr. M. (Mr. Vicecan.) came post hither to ask this vacant office on Wednesday last, & went post to carry the news back on Saturday. the rest were Delaval, Lort, Peck, & Jebb. as to Lort, he deserved it, & Delaval is an honest Gentleman: the rest do me no great honor, no more than my Predecessor did: to be sure, my *Dignity* is a little the worse for wear, but mended & wash'd it will do for me. I am very sincerely

Yours
T G.

To NORTON NICHOLLS

Pemb. Coll. 24 June. 1769.

And so you have a garden of your own, & you plant & transplant & are dirty & amused! are not you ashamed of yourself? Why, I have no such thing, you monster; nor ever shall be either dirty or amused as long as I live! my gardens are in the window, like those of a Lodger up three pair of stairs in Petticoat-lane or Camomile-street, & they go to bed regularly under the same roof that I do. dear, how charming it must be to walk out in one's own garding, & sit on a bench in the open air with a fountain, & a leaden statute, & a rolling stone, & an arbour! have a care of sore-throats tho', & the *agoe.*

Odicle has been rehearsed again & again, & the boys have got scraps by heart: I expect to see it torn piece-meal in the North-Briton, before it is born. The musick is as good as the words: the former might be taken for mine, & the latter for Dr. Randal's. If you will come, you shall see it & sing in it with Mr. Norris, & Mr. Clerke, the Clergyman, and Mr. Reinholt, & Miss Thomas, great names at Salisbury & Gloster musick-meeting, and well-versed in Judas-Maccabæus. Dr. Marriott is to have Lord Sandwich & the Attorney-General at his Lodge, not to mention foreign Ministers, who are to lie with Dr. Hallifax, or in the stables. Lord North is at King's, Lord Weymouth at Mrs. Arbuthnot's, they talk of the D. of Bedford, who (I suppose), has a bed in King's-Chappel. The Archbishop is to be at Christ's, Bishops of London at Clare-Hall, of Lincoln at Dr. Gordon's, of Chester at Peter-House, of Norwich at Jesus, of St. David's at Caius, of Bangor, at the Dog & Porridge-pot, Marq. of Granby at Woodyer's. The Yorkes & Townshends will not come. Soulsby the Taylor lets his room for 11 guineas the 3 days, Woodyer aforesaid for 15. Brotherton asks 20. I have a bed over the way offer'd me at 3 half-crowns a night, but it may be gone, before you come. I believe, all that are unlett will be cheap, as the time approaches. I wish it were once over, & immediately I go for a few days to London, & so (with Mr. Brown) to Aston, tho' I fear it will rain the whole summer, & Skiddaw will be invisible & inaccessible to mortals. I forgot to tell you, that on the Monday (after his Grace has breakfasted on a Divinity-act) twelve Noblemen & Fellowcommoners are to settle his stomach with verses made & repeated by themselves. Saturday next (you know) is the great day, & he goes away on Monday after this repast.

I have got *De la Lande's* Voyage thro' Italy in 8 vols. He is a Member of the Acad. of Sciences, & pretty good to read. I have read an 8vo volume of Shenstone's letters. Poor Man! he was always wishing for money, for fame, & other distinctions, & his whole philosophy consisted in living against his will in retirement, & in a place, which his taste had adorn'd; but which he only enjoy'd, when People of note came to see & commend it. His correspondence is about nothing else but this place & his own writings with two or three neighbouring Clergymen, who wrote verses too.

I will send the Wilton-book directed to Payne for you, tho' I know it will be lost, & then you will say, it was not worth above a shilling, which is a great comfort to me. I have just found the beginning of a letter, which somebody had drop'd: I should rather call it first thoughts for the beginning of a letter, for there are many scratches & corrections. As I can not use it myself (having got a beginning already of my own) I send it for your use upon some great occasion.

Dear Sir

After so long silence the hopes of pardon & prospect of forgiveness might seem entirely extinct or at least very remote, was I not truly sensible of your goodness & candour, which is the only Asylum that my negligence can fly to: since every apology would prove insufficient to counterballance it, or alleviate my fault. How then shall my deficiency presume to make so bold an attempt, or be able to suffer the hardships of so rough a campaign? &c. &c. &c.

And am, Dear Sir

Kindly Yours

T G:

[My] respects to Mrs. Nicholls.

I do not publish at all, but Alma Mater prints 5 or 600 for the company.

I have nothing more to add about Southampton, than what you have transcribed already in your map-book.

To JAMES BROWN

Lancaster, 10 Oct. 1769.

I set out on the 29th September, with poor Doctor Wharton, and lay at Brough, but he was seized with a fit of the asthma the same night, and obliged in the morning to return home. I went by Penrith to Keswick, and passed six days there lap'd in Elysium; then came slowly by Ambleside to Kendal, and this day arrived here. I now am projecting to strike across the hills into Yorkshire, by Settle, and so get to Mason's; then, after a few days, I shall move gently towards Cambridge. The weather has favoured all my motions just as I could wish.

I received your letter of 23 Sept.; was glad you deviated a little from the common track, and rejoiced you got well and safe home.

I am, ever yours

T. G.

To THOMAS WHARTON

Journal

30 Sept. 1769.

Wind at N. W. Clouds & sunshine. A mile & ½ from Brough on a hill lay a great army encamp'd. to the left open'd a fine valley with green meadows & hedge-rows, a Gentleman's house peeping forth from a grove of old trees. On a nearer approach appear'd myriads of horses & cattle in the road itself & in all the fields round me, a brisk stream hurrying cross the way, thousands of clean healthy People in their best party-color'd apparel, Farmers & their families, Esquires & their daughters, hastening up from the dales & down the fells on every side, glittering in the sun & pressing forward to join the throng: while the dark hills, on many of whose tops the mists were yet hanging, served as a contrast to this gay & moving scene, which continued for near two miles more along the road, and the crowd (coming towards it) reach'd on as far as Appleby.

On the ascent of the hill above Appleby the thick hanging wood & the long reaches of the Eden (rapid, clear, & full as ever) winding below with views of the Castle & Town gave much employment to the mirror: but the sun was wanting & the sky overcast. Oats & barley cut every where, but not carried in. Passed Kirby-thore, Sir W. Walston's house at Acorn-bank, Whinfield-park, Harthon-oaks, Countess-pillar, Brougham-Castle, Mr. Brown (one of ye six Clerks) his large new house, cross'd the Eden & the Eimot (pronouce *Eeman*) with its green vale, & at 3 o'clock dined with Mrs. Buchanan, at *Penrith* on trout & partridge. In the afternoon walk'd up the *Beacon-hill* a mile to the top, saw Whinfield and Lowther-parks, & thro' an opening in the bosom of that cluster of mountains, which the Doctor well remembers, the Lake of Ulz-water, with the craggy tops of a hundred nameless hills. These to W. & S., to the N. a great extent of black & dreary plains, to

E. *Cross-fell* just visible thro' mists & vapours hovering round it.

Oct. 1. Wind at S. W. a grey autumnal day, air perfectly calm & gentle. Went to see *Ulz-water* 5 miles distant. Soon left the Keswick-road & turn'd to the left thro' shady lanes along the Vale of *Eeman,* which runs rapidly on near the way, ripling over the stones. To the right is *Delmaine,* a large fabrick of pale red stone with 9 windows in front & 7 on the side built by Mr. Hassel, behind it a fine lawn surrounded by woods & a long rocky eminence rising over them. A clear & brisk rivulet runs by the house to join the Eeman, whose course is in sight & at a small distance.

Farther on appears *Hatton St. John,* a castle-like old mansion of Mr. Huddleston. Approach'd *Dunmallert,* a fine pointed hill, cover'd with wood planted by old Mr. Hassle beforemention'd, who lives always at home & delights in planting. Walk'd over a spungy meadow or two & began to mount this hill thro' a broad & strait green alley among the trees, & with some toil gain'd the summit. From hence saw the Lake opening directly at my feet majestic in its calmness, clear & smooth as a blew mirror with winding shores & low points of land cover'd with green inclosures, white farm-houses looking out among the trees, & cattle feeding. The water is almost every where border'd with cultivated lands gently sloping upwards till they reach the feet of the mountains, which rise very rude & aweful with their broken tops on either hand. Directly in front at better than 3 mile's distance, *Place-Fell,* one of the bravest among them, pushes its bold broad breast into the midst of the Lake & forces it to alter it's course, forming first a large bay to the left & then bending to the right.

I descended *Dunmallert* again by a side avenue, that was only not perpendicular, & came to *Barton*-bridge over the *Eeman,* then walking thro' a path in the wood round the bottom of the hill came forth, where the *Eeman* issues out of the lake, & continued my way along it's western shore close to the water, & generally on a level with it. Saw a cormorant flying over it & fishing. . . . (to be continued)

To THOMAS WHARTON [*1769*]

Aston. 18 Oct. 1769.

Dear Dr.

I hope you got safe and well home after that troublesome night: I long to hear you say so. For me I have continued well, been so favour'd by the weather, that my walks have never once been hinder'd till yesterday, (that is during a fortnight & 3 or 4 days, & a journey of 300 miles, & more) & am now at Aston for two days. Tomorrow I go towards Cambridge: Mason is not here, but Mr. Alderson receives me. My best respects to the family! Adieu! I am ever

Yours (pray, tell me about Stonhewer).

To THOMAS WHARTON

Journal continued

1 Oct. 1769.

The figure of *Ulz-water* nothing resembles that laid down in our maps: it is 9 miles long, & (at widest) under a mile in breadth. After extending itself 3 m. & ½ in a line to S. W. it turns at the foot of *Place-Fell,* almost due West, and is here not twice the breadth of the Thames at London. It is soon again interrupted by the roots of *Helvellyn,* a lofty & very rugged mountain, & spreading again turns off to S. E., & is lost among the deep recesses of the hills. To this second turning I pursued my way about four miles along its borders beyond a village scatter'd among trees & call'd *Water-malloch,* in a pleasant grave day, perfectly calm & warm, but without a gleam of sunshine: then the sky seeming to thicken, the valley to grow more desolate, & evening drawing on, I return'd by the way I came to *Penrith.*

Oct. 2. Wind at S. E., sky clearing, *Cross-fell* misty, but the outline of the other hills very distinct. Set out at 10 for *Keswick,* by the road we went in 1767. Saw *Greystock*-town & castle to the right, which lie only 3 miles (over the Fells) from *Ulz-water.* pass'd through *Penradock* & *Threlcot* at the feet of *Saddleback,* whose furrow'd sides were gilt by the noon-day Sun, while its brow appear'd of a sad purple from the shadow of the clouds, as they sail'd slowly by it. The broad & green valley of *Gardies* and *Low-side,* with a swift stream glittering among the cottages & meadows lay to the left; & the much finer (but narrower) valley of St. *John's* opening into it: *Hill-top* the large, tho' low, mansion of the Gaskarths, now a Farm-house, seated on an eminence among woods under a steep fell, was what appear'd the most conspicuous, & beside it a great rock like some antient tower nodding to its fall. Pass'd by the side of *Skiddaw* & its cub call'd *Latter-rig,* & saw from an eminence at two miles distance the Vale of Elysium in all its verdure, the sun then playing on the bosom of the lake, & lighting up all the mountains with its lustre.

Dined by two o'clock at the Queen's Head, & then straggled out alone to the *Parsonage,* fell down on my back across a dirty lane with my glass open in one hand, but broke only my knuckles: stay'd nevertheless, & saw the sun set in all its glory.

Oct. 3. Wind at S. E., a heavenly day. Rose at seven, & walk'd out under the conduct of my Landlord to *Borrodale.* The grass was cover'd with a hoar-frost, which soon melted, & exhaled in a thin blewish smoke. Cross'd the meadows obliquely, catching a diversity of views among the hills over the lake & islands, & changing prospect at every ten paces, left *Cockshut* & Castle-hill (which we formerly mounted) behind me, & drew near the foot of *Walla-crag,* whose bare & rocky brow, cut perpendicularly down above 400 feet, as I guess, awefully overlooks the way: our path here tends to the left, & the ground gently rising, & cover'd with a glade of scattering trees & bushes on the very margin of the water, opens both ways the most delicious view, that my eyes ever beheld. Behind you are the magnificent heights of *Walla*-crag; opposite lie the thick hanging woods of Lord Egremont, & *Newland*-valley with green & smiling fields embosom'd in the dark cliffs; to the left the jaws of *Borodale,* with that turbulent Chaos of mountain behind mountain roll'd in confusion; beneath you, & stretching far away to the right, the shining purity of the *Lake,* just ruffled by the breeze enough to shew it is alive, reflecting rocks, woods, fields, & inverted tops of mountains, with the white buildings of *Keswick, Crosthwait*-church, & *Skiddaw* for a back-ground at distance. oh Doctor! I never wish'd more for you; & pray think, how the glass played its part in such a spot, which is called *Carf-close-reeds*: I chuse to set down these barbarous names, that any body may enquire on the place, & easily find the particular station, that I mean. This scene continues to *Barrow-gate,* & a little farther, passing a brook called *Barrow-beck,* we enter'd *Borodale.* The crags, named *Lodoor-banks* now begin to impend terribly over your way; & more terribly, when you hear, that three years since an immense mass of rock tumbled at once from the brow, & bar'd all access to the dale (for this is the only road) till they could work their way thro' it. Luckily no one was passing at the time of this fall; but down the side of the mountain & far into the lake lie dispersed the huge fragments of this ruin in all shapes & in all directions. Something farther we turn'd aside into a coppice, ascending a little in front of *Lodoor* water-fall. The height appears to be about 200 feet, the quantity of water not great, tho' (these three days excepted) it had rain'd daily in the hills for near two months before: but then the stream was nobly broken, leaping from rock to rock, & foaming with fury. on one side a towering crag, that spired up to equal, if not overtop, the neighbouring cliffs (this lay all in shade & darkness) on the other hand a rounder broader projecting hill shag'd with wood & illumined by the sun, which glanced sideways on the upper part of the cataract. The force of the water wearing a deep channel in the ground hurries away to join the lake. We descended again, & passed the stream over a rude bridge. Soon after we came under *Gowder-crag,* a hill more formidale to the eye & to the apprehension than that of *Lodoor*; the rocks atop, deep-cloven perpendicularly by the rains, hanging loose & nodding forwards, seem just starting from their base in shivers: the whole way down & the road on both sides is strew'd with piles of the fragments strangely thrown across each other & of a dreadful bulk. The place reminds one of those passes in the Alps, where the Guides tell you to move on with speed, & say nothing, lest the agitation of the air should loosen the snows above, & bring down a mass that would overwhelm a caravan. I took their counsel here and hasten'd on in silence.

Non ragioniam di lor; ma guarda, e passa!
(to be continued)

Dear Dr.

Have you lost the former part of my journal? It was dated from *Aston,* 18 Oct. How does Stonhewer doe? Will his Father's condition allow him to return as yet? I beg my respects to all the family at Old-Park, & am ever

Yours

29 Oct. 1769. Cambridge. T G:

To THOMAS WHARTON

Journal continued

[*Cambridge, November 1769*]

Oct. 3. The hills here are cloth'd all up their steep sides with oak, ash, birch, holly, &c. some of it has been cut 40 years ago, some within these 8 years, yet all is sprung again green, flourishing, & tall for its age, in a place where no soil appears but the staring rock, & where a man could scarce stand upright.

Met a civil young Farmer overseeing his reapers (for it is oat-harvest here) who conducted us to a neat white house in the village of Grange, which is built on a rising ground in the midst of a valley. Round it the mountains form an aweful amphitheatre, & thro' it obliquely runs the Darwent clear as glass, & shewing under it's bridge every trout, that passes. Beside the village rises a round eminence of rock cover'd entirely with old trees, & over that more proudly towers *Castle-crag,* invested also with wood on its sides, & bearing on its naked top some traces of a fort said to be Roman. By the side of this hill, which almost blocks up the way, the valley turns to the left & contracts its dimensions, till there is hardly any road but the rocky bed of the river.

The wood of the mountains increases & their summits grow loftier to the eye, & of more fantastic forms: among them appear *Eagle's-cliff, Dove's-nest, Whitedale-pike,* &c: celebrated names in the annuals of Keswick. The dale opens about four miles higher till you came to *Sea-Whaite* (where lies the way mounting the hills to the right, that leads to the *Wadd-mines*) all farther access is here barr'd to prying Mortals, only there is a little path winding over the Fells, & for some weeks in the year passable to the Dale's-men; but the Mountains know well, that these innocent people will not reveal the mysteries of their ancient kingdom, the reign of Chaos & old Night. Only I learn'd, that this dreadful road dividing again leads one branch to *Ravenglas,* & the other to Hawkshead.

For me I went no farther than the Farmer's (better than 4 m. from Keswick) at *Grange*: his Mother & he brought us butter, that Siserah would have jump'd at, tho' not in a lordly dish, bowls of milk, thin oaten-cakes, & ale; & we had carried a cold tongue thither with us. Our Farmer was himself the Man, that last year plunder'd the Eagle's eirie: all the dale are up in arms on such an occasion, for they lose abundance of lambs yearly, not to mention hares, partridge, grous, &c. He was let down from the cliff in ropes to the shelf of rock, on which the nest was built, the people above shouting & hollowing to fright the old birds, which flew screaming round, but did not dare to attack him. He brought off the eaglet (for there is rarely more than one) & an addle egg. The nest was roundish & more than a yard over, made of twigs twisted together. Seldom a year passes but they take the brood or eggs, & sometimes they shoot one, sometimes the other Parent, but the surviver has always found a mate (probably in Ireland) & they breed near the old place. By his description I learn, that this species is the *Erne* (the Vultur *Albicilla* of Linnæus in his last edition, but in yours *Falco Albicilla*) so consult him & Pennant about it.

Walk'd leisurely home the way we came, but saw a new landscape: the features indeed were the same in part, but many new ones were disclosed by the mid-day Sun, & the tints were entirely changed. Take notice this was the best or perhaps the only day for going up Skiddaw, but I thought it better employ'd: it was perfectly serene, & hot as midsummer.

In the evening walk'd alone down to the Lake by the side of *Crow-Park* after sunset & saw the solemn colouring of night draw on, the last gleam of sunshine fading away on the hill-tops, the deep serene of the waters, & the long shadows of the mountains thrown across them, till they nearly touch'd the hithermost shore. At distance heard the murmur of many waterfalls not audible in the day-time. Wish'd for the Moon, but she was *dark to me & silent, hid in her vacant interlunar cave.*

Oct. 4. Wind E., clouds & sunshine, & in the course of the day a few drops of rain. Walk'd to *Crow-park,* now a rough pasture, once a glade of ancient oaks, whose large roots still remain on the ground, but nothing has sprung from them. If one single tree had remain'd, this would have been an unparallel'd spot, & Smith judged right, when he took his print of the Lake from hence, for it is a gentle eminence, not too high, on the very margin of the water & commanding it from end to end, looking full into the *gorge* of *Borodale.* I prefer it even to *Cockshut-hill,* which lies beside it, & to which I walk'd in the afternoon: it is cover'd with young trees both sown & planted, oak, spruce, scotch-fir, &c. all which thrive wonderfully. There is an easy ascent to the top, & the view far preferable to that on Castle-hill (which you remember) because this is lower & nearer to the Lake: for I find all points, that are much elevated, spoil the beauty of the valley, & make its parts (which are not large) look poor & diminutive. While I was here, a little shower fell, red clouds came marching up the hills from the east, & part of a bright rainbow seem'd to rise along the side of Castle-hill.

From hence I got to the *Parsonage* a little before Sunset, & saw in my glass a picture, that if I could transmitt to you, & fix it in all the softness of its living colours, would fairly sell for a thousand pounds. This is the sweetest scene I can yet discover in point of pastoral beauty. The rest are in a sublimer style.

(to be continued *without end.*)

P. S. I beg your pardon, but I have no franks. The quill arrived very safe, & doubtless is a very snug and commodious method of travelling, for one of the rarities was alive & hearty, & was three times plunged in spirits, before I could get it to die. You are much improved in observation, for a common eye would certainly take it for a pismire. The place of its birth, form of ye antennae, & abdomen, particularly the long *aculeus* under it, shew it to be a *Cynips* (look among the *Hymenoptera*) not yet compleat, for the 4 wings do not appear, that I see. It is not a species described by Linnæus, tho' he mentions others, that breed on the leaves, footstalks, buds, flowers & bark of the Oak. Remember me to Mrs. Wharton & the family. My love to Str., if he has not left Durham. Adieu!

To THOMAS WHARTON

Journal continued

3 Jan. 1770. Pemb. C.

Oct. 5. Wind N. E. Clouds & sunshine. Walk'd thro' the meadows & corn-fields to the Derwent & crossing it went up *How-hill.* It looks along Bassinthwaite-water & sees at the same time the course of the river & a part of the Upper-Lake with a full view of Skiddaw. Then I took my way through Portingskall village to the *Park,* a hill so call'd cover'd entirely with wood: it is all a mass of crumbling slate. Pass'd round its foot between the trees & the edge of the water, & came to a Peninsula that juts out into the lake & looks along it both ways. In front rises Walla-crag, & Castle-hill, the Town, the road to Penrith, Siddaw & Saddleback. Returning met a brisk and cold N. Eastern blast, that ruffled all the surface of ye lake and made it rise in little waves that broke at the foot of the wood. After dinner walked up the Penrith-road 2 miles or more & turning into a corn-field to the right, call'd Castle-Rigg, saw a Druid-Circle of large stones 108 feet in diameter, the biggest not 8 feet high, but most of them still erect: they are

50 in number. The valley of St. John's appear'd in sight, & the summits of *Catchidecam* (called by Camden, *Casticand*) & *Helvellyn,* said to be as high as *Siddaw,* & to rise from a much higher base. A shower came on, & I return'd.

Oct. 6. Wind E. Clouds & sun. went in a chaise 8 miles along the east-side of Bassingth: Water to *Ouse-Bridge* (pronounce *Ews-bridge*) the road in some part made & very good, the rest slippery & dangerous cart-road, or narrow rugged lanes but no precipices: it runs directly along the foot of Skiddaw. Opposite to *Widhope-Brows* (cloth'd to the top with wood) a very beautiful view opens down the Lake, which is narrower & longer than that of Keswick, less broken into bays & without islands. At the foot of it a few paces from the brink gently sloping upward stands *Armathwate* in a thick grove of Scotch firs, commanding a noble view directly up the lake. At a small distance behind the house is a large extent of wood, & still behind this a ridge of cultivated hills, on which (according to the Keswick-proverb) *the Sun always shines.* The inhabitants here on the contrary call the vale of Derwent-water *the Devil's Chamber-pot,* & pronounce the name of *Skiddaw-fell* (which terminates here) with a sort of terror & aversion. *Armathwate-House* is a modern fabrick, not large, & built of dark-red stone, belonging to Mr. *Spedding,* whose Gr.father was Steward to old Sir *Fa. Lowther,* & bought this estate of the *Himers.* So you must look for Mr. Michell in some other country. The sky was overcast & the wind cool, so after dining at a publick house, which stands here near the bridge (that crosses the Derwent just where it issues from the lake) & sauntering a little by the water-side I came home again. The turnpike is finish'd from Cockermouth hither (5 miles) & is carrying on to Penrith. Several little showers to-day. A man came in, who said there was snow on *Cross-fell* this morning.

Oct. 7. Market-day here. Wind N. E. Clouds & Sunshine. little showers at intervals all day. Yet walk'd in the morning to Crow-park, & in the evening up Penrith-road. The clouds came rolling up the mountains all round very [unpromising]; yet the moon shone at intervals. It was too damp to go towards the lake. Tomorrow mean to bid farewell to Keswick.

Botany might be studied here to great advantage at another season because of the great variety of soils & elevations all lieing within a small compass. I observed nothing but several curious Lichens, plenty of gale or Dutch myrtle perfuming the borders of ye lake. This year the Wadd mine had been open'd (which is done once in 5 years) it is taken out in lumps sometimes as big as a man's fist & will undergo no preparation by fire, not being fusible. When it is pure soft, black, & close-grain'd, it is worth sometimes 30 shillings a pound. There are no Charr ever taken in these lakes, but plenty in Butter-mere-water, which lies a little way N. of Borrodale, about Martlemas, which are potted here. They sow chiefly oats & bigg here, which are now cutting, & still on the ground. The rains have done much hurt; yet observe, the soil is so thin & light, that no day has pass'd, in which I could not walk out with ease, & you know, I am no lover of dirt. Fell-mutton is now in season for about six weeks; it grows fat on ye mountains, & nearly resembles venison: excellent Pike & Perch (here called *Bass*) trout is out of season. Partridge in great plenty.

Receipt to dress Perch (for Mrs. Wharton)

Wash, but neither scale, nor gut them. Broil till enough; then pull out the fins, & open them along ye back, take out the bone & all the inwards without breaking them. Put in a large lump of butter & salt, clap the sides together, till it melts, & serve very hot. It is excellent. The skin must not be eaten.

Oct. 8. Left Keswick & took the Ambleside-road in a gloomy morning. Wind E. & N. E. About 2 m. from the Town mounted an eminence call'd *Castle-rigg,* & the sun breaking out discover'd the most enchanting view I have yet seen of the whole valley behind me, the two lakes, the river, the mountains all in their glory! had almost a mind to have gone back again. The road in some few parts is not compleated, but good country-road thro' sound, but narrow & stony lanes, very safe in broad day-light. This is the case about *Causeway-foot* & among Naddle-Fells to *Lanewaite.* The vale you go in has little breadth, the mountains are vast & rocky, the fields little & poor, & the inhabitants are now making hay, & see not the sun by two hours in a day so long as at Keswick. Came to the foot of Helvellyn along which runs an excellent road, looking down from a little height on *Lee's water* (call'd also Thirl-meer, or Wiborn-water & soon descending on its margin. The lake from its depth looks black (tho' really clear as glass) & from the gloom of the vast crags, that scowl over it: it is narrow & about 3 miles long, resembling a river in its course. Little shining torrents hurry down the rocks to join it, with not a bush to overshadow them, or cover their march. All is rock & loose stones up to the very brow, which lies so near your way, that not half the height of Helvellyn can be seen. . . (to be continued, but now we have got franks)

Happy new year & many to you all. Hepatica & Mezereon now in flower! I saw Mrs. Jonathan, who is much fallen away, & was all in tears for the loss of her Brother's child: she & Miss Wilson desired their compliments. Your nephew is here & very well. So is Mr. Brown, who presents his best wishes.

Continuation of Journal

Past by the little Chappel of Wiborn, out of which the Sunday-congregation were then issuing.

Past a beck near *Dunmail-raise,* & enter'd *Westmoreland* a second time. Now begin to see *Helm-Crag* distinguish'd from its rugged neighbours not so much by its height, as by the strange broken outline of its top, like some gigantic building demolish'd, & the stones that composed it, flung cross each other in wild confusion. Just beyond it opens one of the sweetest landscapes, that art ever attempted to imitate. (the bosom of ye mountains spreading here into a broad bason) discovers in the midst Grasmere-water. Its margin is hollow'd into small bays with bold eminences some of rock, some of soft turf, that half conceal, and vary the figure of the little lake they command, from the shore a low promontory pushes itself far into the water, & on it stands a white village with the parish-church rising in the midst of it, hanging enclosures, corn-fields, & meadows green as an emerald with their trees & hedges & cattle fill up the whole space from the edge of the water & just opposite to you is a large farm-house at the bottom of a steep smooth lawn embosom'd in old woods, which climb half way up the mountain's side, & discover above them a broken line of crags, that crown the scene. Not a single red tile, no flaring Gentleman's house, or garden-walls, break in upon the repose of this unsuspected paradise, but all is peace, rusticity, & happy poverty in its neatest most becoming attire.

The road winds here over *Grasmere-hill,* whose rocks soon conceal the water from your sight, yet it is continued along behind them, & contracting itself to a river communicates with Ridale-water, another small lake, but of inferior size & beauty. It seems shallow too, for large patches of reeds appear pretty far within it. Into this vale the road descends.. On the opposite banks large & ancient woods mount up the hills, & just to the left of our way stands *Rydale*-hall, the family-seat of Sir Mic. Fleming, but now a farm-house, a large old-fashion'd fabrick surrounded with wood & not much too good for its present destination. Sir Michael is now on his travels, & all this timber far & wide belongs to him. I tremble for it, when he returns. Near the house rises a huge crag call'd *Rydale-head,* which is said to command a full view of Wynandermere, & I doubt it not, for within a mile that great Lake is visible even from the road. As to going up the crag one might as well go up Skiddaw.

Came to Ambleside, 18 m. from Keswick meaning to lie there, but on looking into the best bed-chamber dark & damp as a cellar grew delicate, gave up Winandermere in despair & resolved I would go on to *Kendal* directly, 14 m. farther. The road in general fine turnpike, but some parts (about 3 m. in all) not made, yet without danger.

Unexpectedly was well-rewarded for my determination, the afternoon was fine, & the road for full 5 m. runs along the side of Winder-mere with delicious views across it & almost from one end to the other. It is ten miles in length, & at most a mile over, resembling the course of some vast & magnificent river, but no flat marshy grounds, no osier-beds, or patches of scrubby plantation on its banks. At the head two vallies open among the mountains, one that by which we came down, the other *Langsledale,* in which *Wreenose & Hard-Knot,* two great mountains, rise above the rest. From thence the fells visibly sink & soften along its sides, sometimes they run into it (but with a gentle declivity) in their own dark & natural complexion, oftener they are green & cultivated with farms interspersed & round eminences on the border cover'd with trees: towards the South it seem'd to break into larger bays with several islands & a wider extent of cultivation. The way rises continually till at a place call'd *Orrest-head* it turns to S.E. losing sight of the water.

Pass'd by *Ings-Chappel,* & *Staveley,* but I can say no farther, for the dusk of evening coming on I enter'd *Kendal* almost in the dark & could distinguish only a shadow of the Castle on a hill, & tenter-grounds spread far & wide round the Town, which I mistook for houses. My inn promised sadly having two wooden galleries (like Scotland) in front of it. It was indeed an old ill-contrived house, but kept by civil sensible people, so I stay'd two nights with them & fared & slept very comfortably.

Oct. 9. Wind N.W. Clouds & sun. Air mild as summer. All corn off the ground, sky-larks singing aloud (by the way I saw not one at Keswick, perhaps because the place abounds in birds of prey). Went up the Castle-hill. The Town consists chiefly of three nearly parallel streets almost a mile long. Except these all the other houses seem as if they had been dancing a country-dance & were out: there they stand back to back, corner to corner, some up hill, some down without intent or meaning. Along by their side runs a fine brisk stream, over which are 3 stone-bridges. The buildings (a few comfortable houses excepted) are mean, of stone & cover'd with a bad rough-cast. Near the end of the Town stands a handsome house of Col. Wilson's & adjoining to it the Church, a very large Gothic fabrick with a square Tower. It has no particular ornaments but double isles, & at the east-end 4 chappels, or choirs.

One of the *Pars,* another of the *Stricklands,* the 3d is the proper choir of ye church, & the 4th of ye *Bellingcams,* a family now extinct. There is an altar-tomb of one of them dated 1577 with a flat brass, arms & quarterings & in the window their arms alone, Arg. a hunting-horn, sab. strung Gules. In the *Strickland's* chappel several modern monuments, & another old altar-tomb, not belonging to the family: on the side of it, a Fess dancetty between 10 Billets (Deincourt?) in the *Parr*-chappel is a third altar-tomb in the corner, no fig. or inscription, but on the side cut in stone an escutcheon of *Roos* of Kendal (3 Water-Budgets) quartering *Parr* (2 bars in a bordure engrail'd). 2dly an escutcheon, Vaire, a Fess (for Marmion). 3dly an escutcheon. three Chevronels braced & a Chief (which I take for Fitzhugh) at the foot is an escutcheon surronded with the Garter, bearing *Roos* & *Parr* quarterly, quartering the other two beforemention'd. I have no books to look in, therefore can not say, whether this is the Lord *Parr of Kendal* (Queen Catharine's Father) or her Brother, the Marquis of *Northampton.* It is a Cenotaph for the latter, who was buried at Warwick in 1571. The remains of the Castle are seated on a fine hill on the side of the river opposite to the Town. Almost the whole enclosure of walls remains with 4 towers, 2 square & 2 or 3 round, but their upper part & embattlements are demolished. It is of rough stone & cement, without any ornament or arms, round enclosing a court of like form & surrounded by a mote, nor ever could have been larger than it is, for there are no traces of outworks. There is a good view of the town & river with a fertile open valley, thro which it winds.

After dinner went along the Milthrop-turnpike 4 m. to see the falls (or force) of the river *Kent.* Came to *Siserge* (pronounce Siser) & turn'd down a lane to the left. Siser, the seat of the *Stricklands* an old Catholick family, is an ancient Hall-house, with a very large tower embattled: the rest of the buildings added to this are of later date, but all is white & seen to advantage on a back ground of old trees: there is a small park also well-wooded. Opposite to this turn'd to the left & soon came to the river. It works its way in a narrow & deep rocky channel o'erhung with trees. The calmness & brightness of ye evening, the roar of the waters, & the thumping of huge hammers at an iron-forge not far distant made it a singular walk, but as to the falls (for there are two) they are not 4 feet high. I went on down to the forge & saw the Dæmons at work by the light of their own fires: the iron is brought in pigs to Milthrop by sea from Scotland &c. & is here beat into bars & plates. Two miles farther at *Levens* is the seat of Lord Suffolk, where he sometimes passes the summer. It was a favourite place of his late Countess: but this I did not see.

Oct. 10. went by *Burton* to Lancaster. Wind N. W. Clouds & sun. 22 m. Very good country well enclosed & wooded with some common interspersed. Pass'd at the foot of *Farlton-Knot*, a high fell. 4 N. of Lancaster on a rising ground call'd *Bolton* (pron. *Bouton*)*-Wait* had a full view of *Cartmell-sands* with here and there a Passenger riding over them (it being low water) the points of Furness shooting far into the sea, & lofty mountains partly cover'd with clouds extending North of them. Lancaster also appear'd very conspicuous & fine, for its most dinstinguish'd features the Castle & Church, mounted on a green eminence, were all, that could be seen. Woe is me! when I got thither, it was the second day of the fair. The Inn (in the principal street) was a great old gloomy house full of people, but I found tolerable quarters, & even slept two nights in peace.

Ascended the Castle-hill in a fine afternoon. It takes up the higher top of the eminence on which it stands, & is irregularly round, encompassed with a deep mote. In front towards the Town is a magnificent Gothick Gateway, lofty & huge, the overhanging battlements are supported by a triple range of corbels, the intervals pierced thro' & shewing the day from above. On its top rise light watchtowers of small height. It opens below with a grand pointed arch: over this is a wrought tabernacle, doubtless once containing the Founders figure, on one side a shield of France semy quarter'd with England, on the other the same with a label ermine for John of Gant D. of Lancaster. This opens to a court within, which I did not much care to enter, being the County Gaol & full of Prisoners, both Criminals & Debtors. From this gateway the walls continue & join it to a vast square tower of great height, the lower part at least of remote antiquity, for it has small round-headed lights with plain short pillars on each side of them, there is a third tower also square & of less dimensions. This is all the castle, near it & but little lower stands the Church, a large & plain Gothic fabrick, the high square Tower at the West-end has been rebuilt of late years, but nearly in the same style. There are no ornaments of arms, &c. any where to be seen. Within it is lightsome & spacious, but not one monument of antiquity, or piece of painted glass is left. From the Church-yard there is an extensive sea-view (for now the tide had almost cover'd the sands, & fill'd the river) & besides greatest part of Furness I could distinguish *Pell*-Castle on the isle of Fowdrey, which lies off its southern extremity. The Town is built on the slope & at the feet of the Castle-hill more than twice the bigness of Aukland with many neat buildings of white stone, but a little disorderly in their position ad libitum like Kendal. Many also extend below on the keys by the river-side, where a number of ships were moor'd, some of them three-mast vessels deck'd out with their colours in honor of the Fair. Here is a good bridge of 4 arches over the *Lune,* which runs (when the tide is out) in two streams divided by a bed of gravel, which is not cover'd but in spring-tides. Below the town it widens to near the breadth of ye Thames at London, & meets the sea at 5 or 6 m. distance to S.W.

Oct. 11. Wind S.W. Clouds & sun. Warm & a fine dappled sky. Cross'd the river & walk'd over a peninsula 3 miles to the village of *Pooton* which stands on the beach. An old Fisherman mending his nets (while I enquired about the danger of passing those sands) told me in his dialect a moving story, how a brother of the trade, a *Cockler* (as he styled him) driving a little cart with two daughters (women grown) in it, & his Wife on horseback following, set out one day to pass the 7 mile sands, as they had frequently been used to do, for nobody in the village knew them better than the old Man did. When they were about half way over, a thick fog rose, & as they advanced, they found the water much deeper than they expected. The old man was puzzled, he stop'd & said he would go a little way to find some mark he was acquainted with. They staid a little while for him, but in vain. They call'd aloud, but no reply. At last the young women press'd their mother to think, where they were, & go on. She would not leave the place, she wander'd about forlorn & amazed, she would not quit her horse, & get into the cart with them. They determined after much time wasted to turn back, & give themselves up to the guidance of their horses. The old Woman was soon wash'd off and perish'd. The poor Girls clung close to their cart, & the horse sometimes wading & sometimes swimming brought them back to land alive, but senseless with terror & distress & unable for many days to give any account of themselves. The bodies of their parents were found soon after, that of the Father a very few paces distant from the spot, where he had left them.

In the afternoon wander'd about the town & by the key till it grew dark. a little rain fell.

Oct. [12] Wind N.E. Sky gloomy, then gleams of sunshine. Set out for *Settle* by a fine turnpike road, 29 miles.

Rich & beautiful enclosed country diversified with frequent villages & churches, very unequal ground, & on the left the river Lune winding in a deep valley, its hanging banks clothed with fine woods, thro' which you catch long reaches of the water, as the road winds about at a considerable height above it. Pass'd the *Park* (Hon. Mr. Clifford's, a catholick) in the most picturesque part of the way. The grounds between him & the river are indeed charming: the house is ordinary, & the park nothing but a rocky fell scatter'd over with ancient hawthorns. Came to *Hornby* a little Town on the river Wanning, over which a handsome bridge is now in building. The Castle in a lordly situation attracted me, so I walked up the hill to it. First presents itself a large but ordinary white Gentleman's house sash'd. Behind it rises the ancient Keep built by Edward Stanley, Lord Mounteagle (inscribed Helas et quand?) he died about 1524 in Henry the 8th's time. It is now a shell only, tho' rafters are laid within it as for flooring. I went up a winding stone-staircase in one corner to the leads, & at the angle is a single hexagon watch-tower rising some feet higher, fitted up in the tast of a modern *Toot* with sash-windows in gilt frames, & a stucco cupola, & on the top a vast eagle by Mr. *Charteris,* the present Professor. But he has not lived here since the year 1745, when the people of Lancaster insulted him, threw stones into his coach, & almost made his Wife (Lady Katherine Gordon) miscarry. Since that he has built a great ugly house of red stone (thank God it is not in England) near Haddington, which I remember to have pass'd by. He is the 2d Son of the Earl of Wemyss, & brother to the Lord Elcho, Grandson to Col. Charteris, whose name he bears.

From the leads of the Tower there is a fine view of the country round, & much wood near the castle. Ingleborough, which I had seen before distinctly at Lancaster to N.E. was now compleatly wrap'd in clouds all but its summit, which might have been easily mistaken for a long black cloud too, fraught with an approaching storm. Now our road begun gradually to mount towards the *Apennine,* the trees growing less, and thinner of leaves, till we came to Ingleton 18 m. It is a pretty village situated very high & yet in a valley at the foot of that huge creature of God *Ingleborough.* Two torrents cross it with great stones roll'd along their bed instead of water: over them are two handsome arches flung. here at a little ale-house where Sr. Bellingcam Graham & Mr. Parker Lord of ye Manour (one of them 6 feet ½ high, & the other as much in breadth) come to dine.

The nipping air (tho' the afternoon was growing very bright) now taught us, we were in Craven. The road was all up & down (tho' no where very steep). To the left were mountain-tops (Weryside), to the right a wide valley (all inclosed ground) & beyond it high hills again. In approaching Settle the crags on the left drew nearer to our way, till we ascend *Brunton-brow,* into a chearful valley (tho' thin of trees) to *Giggleswick* a village with a small piece of water by its side cover'd over with coots.

Near it a Church, which belongs also to *Settle* & half a mile father having passed the *Ribble* over a bridge arrived at *Settle.* It is a small market-town standing directly under a rocky fell. There are not a dozen good-looking houses, the rest are old & low with little wooden portico's in front. My inn pleased me much (tho' small) for the neatness & civility of the good Woman that kept it, so I lay there two nights, & went

Oct. [13] to visit *Gordale-Scar.* Wind N.E. Day gloomy & cold. It lay but 6 m. from Settle, but that way was directly over a Fell, & it might rain, so I went round in a chaise the only way one could get near it in a carriage, which made it full 13 m. & half of it such a road! but I got safe over it, so there's an end, & came to *Malham* (pronounce *Maum*) a village in the bosom of the mountains seated in a wild & dreary valley. From thence I was to walk a mile over a very rough ground, a torrent rattling along on the left hand. On the cliffs above hung a few goats: one of them danced & scratched an ear with its hind-foot in a place where I would not have stood stock-still

for all beneath the moon.

As I advanced the crags seem'd to close in, but discover'd a narrow entrance turning to the left between them. I followed my guide a few paces, & lo, the hills open'd again into no large space, & then all farther way is bar'd by a stream, that at the height of about 50 feet gushes from a hole in the rock, & spreading in large sheets over its broken front dashes from steep to steep, & then rattles away in a torrent down the valley. The rock on the left rises perpendicular with stubbed yew-trees & shrubs, staring from its side to the height of at least 300 feet. But these are not the thing! it is that to the right, under which you stand to see the fall, that forms the principal horror of the place. From its very base it begins to slope forwards over you in one black & solid mass without any crevice in its surface, & overshadows half the area below with its dreadful canopy. When I stood at (I believe) full 4 yards distance from its foot, the drops which perpetually distill from its brow, fell on my head, & in one part of the top more exposed to the weather there are loose stones that hang in air, & threaten visibly some idle Spectator with instant destruction. It is safer to shelter yourself close to its bottom, & trust the mercy of that enormous mass, which nothing but an earthquake can stir. The gloomy uncomfortable day well suited the savage aspect of the place, & made it still more formidable. I stay'd there (not without shuddering) a quarter of an hour, & thought my trouble richly paid, for the impression will last for life. At the alehouse where I dined, in Malham, Vivares, the landscape-painter, had lodged for a week or more. Smith & Bellers had also been there, & two prints of Gordale have been engraved by them. Return'd to my comfortable inn. Night fine, but windy & frosty.

Oct. [14]. Went to Skipton, 16 miles. Wind N.E. gloomy, at one o'clock a little sleet falls. From several parts of the road, & in many places about Settle I saw at once the three famous hills of this country, Ingleborough, Penigent, & Pendle, the first is esteem'd the highest. their features are hard to describe, but I could trace their outline with a pencil.

Craven after all is an unpleasing country, when seen from a height. Its valleys are chiefly wide & either marshy, or enclosed pasture with a few trees. Numbers of black Cattle are fatted here, both of the Scotch breed, & a larger sort of oxen with great horns. There is little cultivated ground, except a few oats.

[Oct. 14. Wind N.E. gloomy. At noon a few grains of sleet fell, then bright & clear. Went thro' Long-Preston & Gargrave to] *Skipton* [16 miles. It] is a pretty large Market-Town in a valley with one very broad street gently sloping downwards from the Castle, which stands at the head of it. This is one of our good Countesse's buildings, but on old foundations: it is not very large, but of a handsome antique appearance with round towers, a grand Gateway, bridge & mote, & many old trees about it, in good repair, & kept up, as a habitation of the Earl of Thanet, tho' he rarely comes thither. What with the sleet & a foolish dispute about chaises, that delay'd me, I did not see the inside of it, but went on 15 miles to *Ottley*. First up *Shodebank,* the steepest hill I ever saw a road carried over in England, for it mounts in a strait line (without any other repose for the horses, than by placing stones every now & then behind the wheels) for a full mile. Then the road goes on a level along the brow of this high hill over Rumbald-moor, till it gently descends into *Wharldale*: so they call the Vale of the Wharf, & a beautiful vale it is, well-wooded, well-cultivated, well-inhabited, but with high crags at distance, that border the green country on either hand. Thro' the midst of it deep, clear, full to the brink, & of no inconsiderable breadth runs in long windings the river. How it comes to pass that it should be so fine & copious a stream here, & at Tadcaster (so much lower) should have nothing but a wide stony channel without water, I can not tell you. I pass'd through *Long-Addingham, Ilkeley* (pronounce *Eecla*) distinguish'd by a lofty brow of loose rocks to the right, *Burley,* a neat & pretty village among trees. On the opposite side of the river lay *Middleton*-Lodge, belonging to a Catholick Gentleman of that name; *Weston,* a venerable stone-fabrick with large offices, of Mr. Vavasor, the meadows in front gently descending to the water, & behind a great & shady wood. Farnley (Mr. Fawke's) a place like the last, but larger, & rising higher on the side of the hill. *Ottley* is a large airy Town, with clean but low rustick buildings, & a bridge over the Wharf. I went into its spatious Gothic Church, which has been new-roof'd with a flat stucco ceiling. In a corner of it is the monument of Tho. Lord Fairfax, & Helen Aske, his Lady, descended from the Cliffords & Latimers, as her epitaph says. The figures not ill-cut particularly his in armour, but bare-headed, lie on the tomb. I take them for the Grand Parents of the famous Sr. Tho. Fairfax.

To HORACE WALPOLE

[*Cambridge*], *March 17, 1771.*

. . . He must have a very good stomach that can digest the *Crambe recocta* of Voltaire. Atheism is a vile dish, tho' all the cooks of France combine to make new sauces to it. As to the Soul, perhaps they may have none on the Continent; but I do think we have such things in England. Shakespear, for example, I believe had several to his own share. As to the Jews (tho' they do not eat pork) I like them because they are better Christians than Voltaire. . . .

To NORTON NICHOLLS

Jermyn-Street. 28 June, 1771.

Dear Sir

The inclosed came a few days after you left us, as I apprehend, from Temple. I continue here much against my will. The gout is gone, the feverish disorder abated, but not cured; my spirits much oppress'd, & the more so, as I foresee a new complaint, that may tie me down perhaps to my bed, & expose me to the operations of a Surgeon. God knows, what will be the end of it.

It will be an alleviation to my miseries, if I can hear, you are well, & capable of enjoying those objects of curiosity, that the countries you are in promise to afford you. The greater the detail you give me of them, the happier I shall be. Mr. Clarke call'd on me yesterday, & desires to be remember'd. I know nothing new here, but that Mr. T. Pitt is going to be married to a Miss Wilkinson, the daughter of a rich Merchant, who gives her 30,000£ down, & at least as much more in expectation. Adieu! I am faithfully

Yours

T G:

Wilkes is like to lose his election.

INDEX

An italicized page reference indicates a letter from Gray.